MEMOIR
YOUR
WAY

Tell Your Story through Writing, Recipes, Quilts, Graphic Novels, and More

THE MEMOIR ROUNDTABLE

Skyhorse Publishing

Skyhorse Publishing books may be purchased in bulk at special discounts for sales promotion, corporate gifts, fund-raising, or educational purposes. Special editions can also be created to specifications. For details, contact the Special Sales Department, Skyhorse Publishing, 307 West 36th Street, 11th Floor, New York, NY 10018 or info@skyhorsepublishing.com.

Skyhorse® and Skyhorse Publishing® are registered trademarks of Skyhorse Publishing, Inc.®, a Delaware corporation.

Visit our website at www.skyhorsepublishing.com.

10 9 8 7 6 5 4 3 2 1

Library of Congress Cataloging-in-Publication Data is available on file.

Cover design by Jane Sheppard
Cover photo credit: iStockphoto

Print ISBN: 978-1-5107-0751-1
Ebook ISBN: 978-1-5107-0752-8

Printed in China

CONTENTS

MEET THE AUTHORS

Back row, l-r: Natasha Peterson, Linda Pool, Joanne Lozar Glenn; front row, l-r: Nadine James, Katherine Nutt, Dianne Hennessy King

The Memoir Roundtable is a group of six writers, crafters, and workshop leaders: nationally known quilter and American Folk Art Museum award winner Linda Pool; public TV producer, cookbook editor, and cultural anthropologist Dianne Hennessy King; award-winning writer and memoir workshop leader Joanne Lozar Glenn; children's literacy expert and speaker Nadine James; memoir teacher, educational game inventor, and scrapper Katherine Nutt; and award-winning content producer, author, and graphic novel creator Natasha Peterson. The authors reside in Virginia.

Chapter 1
MEMOIR YOUR WAY

A memoir can take many forms. After all, it is

your story, your way.

If you are ready to create a memoir, but not so sure how to get started, then *Memoir Your Way* is meant for you. We say scrap it, quilt it, write it, or cook it up so the family can have a tangible piece of their heritage. After all, it is your story, your way. And there are many ways to tell your story.

Crafting a memoir—whether a cookbook of family recipes, a scrapbook, a memory quilt, a slice of life told in a series of drawings or collages, or a homemade video interview with a family elder—can be surprisingly satisfying. By bringing our memories into the world in a concrete form, we can step back and see our experiences in a different, and often healing, light. The last word, the last stitch, the last drop of glue can open the door to a whole new way of seeing and even being.

Beyond the surprise and satisfaction, though, is the larger value—your contribution to the family legacy. By telling your story, you bring to life the parents and grandparents, aunts and uncles, siblings and cousins that future little ones will never know. We're all in this joyful, fascinating, sometimes scary adventure of being a witness to our lives and the lives of our families. If we don't remember their stories, who will? If we don't tell their stories, how will they live in history? When we turn our memories into memoir, we build the bridge between the past and the future.

Turning Memories into Memoir

Many people want to preserve family memories but don't think they have the time or the energy for such a daunting task. Breathe easy! Creating a memoir can be easier than you think.

Here's why: A memoir does not have to include *everything* about a life. In fact, it shouldn't. There is no "A" (for autobiography) in m-e-m-o-i-r! (Neither is there a "B" for biography!) You can let go of the idea that your memoir must include every life event that you—or the person or family you're memorializing—experienced.

Credit: *Emily Roesly.*

Turn memories into memoir. We're all in this joyful, fascinating, sometimes scary adventure of being a witness to our lives and the lives of our families. When we turn our memories into memoir, we build the bridge between the past and the future.

So if memoirs are not autobiography or biography, what exactly are they?

In other words, what makes a memory, or a group of memories, a memoir?

Here's a sketch that answers part of that question.

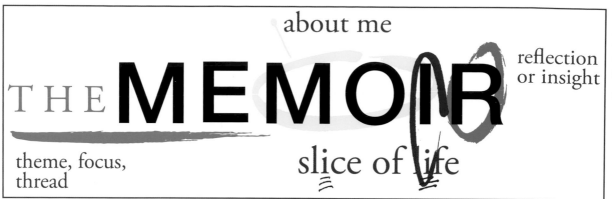

Memoir is a slice of life. A memoir is always two stories—the story of what happened, and the meaning we make of it.

Okay, let's debrief.

First, memoir is a slice of life. Any of us can write more than one memoir, because we have multi-dimensional lives. You could create a memoir about your life as a parent, or a memoir that represents your career, or a memoir about your divorce.

Secondly, that slice of life has a theme that links individual stories together. You can think of a theme as a focusing idea or a "thread" that runs through the tapestry of your life. Here are a few examples:

- A talented cook decides to assemble a cookbook of recipes commemorating her "mixed" culinary heritage (she is both Jewish and Italian). The recipes will be for foods eaten to celebrate Jewish and Italian holidays, and will include brief stories about the relatives who gave her the recipes, including a story about the weathered wooden spoon she inherited from her grandmother. Notice that she does not include a recipe for her famous sweet-potato French fries, because that doesn't fit the theme.

- A man dies in an accident. His sister decides to use scraps of his clothing in a quilt that will memorialize his life and be a keepsake for his son.
- A Navy officer decides to write a memoir about struggles she faced on her way to becoming one of the first female pilots in that service. The "thread" is everything that connects to being a female pilot in a male-dominated field, including the frustrations and triumphs.

Finally, because memories involve "looking backward," a memoir involves reflection and possibly an insight or "life lesson"–what you learned as a result of your experience, the kind of story you might tell at the kitchen table to a friend while the two of you are sipping tea or to one of your children while you are doing chores together. The reflective aspect of memoir lets us make sense of life events and often reveals how we changed or grew in our understanding of ourselves. Often it gives us a deeper understanding of others.

Remember that a memoir is always two stories–what happened or what is remembered, and what it meant to you or to the person whose story you are telling. The memoir could be as sweeping as escaping a war or as enchantingly small as "the day we met."

Starting Where You Are

The advantage of using this book as a guide to creating your memoir is that you can start where you are with what you know, the materials you have at hand, and the approach that appeals to you most.

If you want to write your family stories, for example, you'll find help in chapter 2. If you want to try a memoir quilt, you'll find guidance in chapter 6.

If, like the woman of mixed culinary heritage, you want to put together a cookbook memoir, you'll find step-by-step directions in chapter 3. If scrapbooking is more your style, see chapter 4 for how-to tips, including using online resources to create digital scrapbooks. If you are an artist or illustrator, see chapter 5 for examples of graphic-novel-style memoirs. And don't forget that your kids are natural storytellers—see chapter 7 for ideas on how to get them involved in creating a family memoir by interviewing relatives about slices of their lives.

Sometimes the stories you discover will make you want to know more about your heritage than you have been told. In this case, research might be involved. Chapter 8 offers resources you can use to "fill in the blanks."

Working It Through

No matter what form you choose for your memoir, you'll probably follow similar steps:

1. Decide your goal.
2. Gather your materials, including the artifacts you want to work with.
3. Decide what theme or focus you want your memoir to have.
4. Decide on a suitable arrangement or organization.
5. Supplement with research, photographs, or whatever you need to complete your vision.
6. Branch off to whatever chapter in this book best allows you to create your memoir your way, so you can create your finished product.

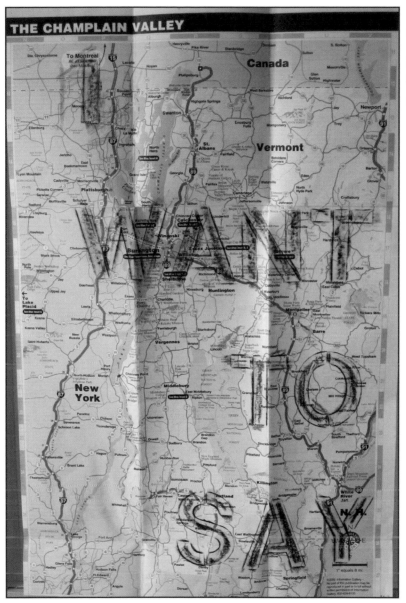

Start where you are. The important thing is to "capture" the story. Make it exist in a form you can look at, hold, listen to, or even taste over and over again.

Start small for a quick feeling of accomplishment. Then as you become more comfortable, expand your goals. Whatever you learn in completing a "mini-memoir" you can always transfer to a bigger project.

The important thing is to "capture" the story from where it might be hiding—in your memory or someone else's, in the boxes in the basement—and put the pieces together. Make the story exist in a form you can look at, hold, listen to, or even taste over and over again. Don't worry about whether it would win an award. Its value lies in creating it in the first place. When you do this—and *do* is the key word here—the story becomes more real. You understand it better. You can share it and pass it along to others who can do the same. It, like you, is unique—and priceless.

Keep in Mind

There are many ways to tell your story. Choose the format that is most pleasing to you.

- Crafting a memoir can be not only surprising and satisfying, but a way to bridge the past and the future.
- Memoir is a slice of life remembered and reflected upon. It is always two stories: the memory, and the meaning we make of it.
- Start where you are, and supplement what you have with artifacts or research to create a memoir that is uniquely your own—and therefore priceless.

FAQs: Making a Memoir

Here are three questions people who are working on a memoir typically ask.

Q: What if I can't remember the story details?

A: You don't have to—not completely, anyway. Just get started. You will be amazed how jotting down notes about your story will trigger memories you thought were long gone. You know that expression "It's all coming back now"? Once you begin to focus on your story, that part of your brain kicks into gear, and memories, like the way a room looked, or the weather outside, start spilling forth. Your stories are already there in your head and your heart waiting for you to choose your form of expression and dive in. And remember: you can always do some research, whether that research involves interviewing a relative or searching the internet.

Q: How do I handle family secrets?

A: There are no hard and fast rules, but consider a few guidelines before forging ahead. First, tell your story your way, heart and soul, the first time around before making it "public." When you review your project, you can decide to change names or add or omit certain details. You can also ask yourself whether the secret is important to your story. For example, if you are creating a family cookbook and you discover that your grandmother was married once before she met your grandfather, is that really important to include? If her first husband was a chef and taught her all she knew, then maybe it is. But if she was very young

9

when she married, and the marriage fell apart after six weeks, it might have no place in a family legacy cookbook.

In the end, it's your memory and your story. We all remember things differently. Sarah Polley tackled this issue in her documentary film, *Stories We Tell*, an exploration of the truth about her paternity. She suggested that the stories we tell, even in the same family, will never entirely agree.

Q: What if some of my stories are sad or depressing, or about struggle rather than success?

A: That's called being true to life. Tell the sad and the glad stories. By including both, you introduce an element of contrast, which works really well in storytelling and in art. Think of what makes an image interesting: the dark and light colors, the highs and lows of each tone. If your memoir projects are unified by theme, your slice-of-life memoir will feel complete and honest precisely *because* you included the ups and the downs, the successes and the struggles.

Chapter 2
FIVE SIMPLE STEPS TO TELLING A TRUE STORY

— *By Joanne Lozar Glenn* —

Once you start creating your memoir, what do you do with all the memories that come flooding in? The answer is be selective, and tell the truest story you can.

The quilt, scrapbook, cookbook, and other forms of memoir described in this book are even more special when you add your own story, told in your own words. Once you start telling that story, though, you might be surprised at the flood of memories a simple *Memoir Your Way* project can unleash. Now that you've got all these memories, what do you do with them?

You'll find some ideas here. In this chapter, you'll learn to "write small," using a few key techniques that will sharpen the focus of what you're writing and make your story come alive.

Try these five simple steps to create a memoir that is not just memories, but memorable . . . one your audience won't forget.

1. Choose a Moment

Writer and humorist Anne Lamott offers good advice for any writer tackling a writing project: keep the focus small—small enough to fit in a one-inch picture frame. Here's what she means: write deep rather than wide.

And what does "deep rather than wide" mean? Glad you asked! Instead of writing down *everything* that happened to you in second grade, say, write extensively and deeply about one moment in second grade that you still remember to this day. It could be the time you learned how to swing a pail full of water without spilling a drop (you discovered centrifugal force!) or the day you stood up to a bully (you never let anyone bully you—or anyone else—again!).

Why is it important to write deep rather than wide? Because writing becomes more interesting—and has more impact—as it becomes more specific. There's nothing wrong, for example, with captioning an old black-and-white photo like this:

My father packed the car for our trip to the lake.

PHOTO BY *Rachel Cowan.*

Keep the focus small. Think of writing only as much as will fill a one-inch picture frame. Write extensively and deeply about a moment you still remember to this day. The more specific the details, the more interesting and impactful the writing.

But if you write this—

My father packed our blue '63 Buick with a Coleman cooler filled with hot dogs and my mom's homemade sauerkraut.

—you give details that show the time period, and your readers also associate smells and tastes with your story. They are *there with you.*

If you wonder which moments to write about, consider using the turning points of your life. These can be moments that haunt you or memories you carry around like a blanket that warms you on a cold night. They are often the moments in life that we remember with keepsakes or other ways of memorializing what happened. A family I know, for example, wears black wristbands to remember a child who died. The family storykeeper could decide to attach a black wristband to the scrapbook page, along with a story about what happened and why the family chose black wristbands as a remembrance. This scrapbook memoir then becomes a gift to future generations, because it makes the child who died real for the young family members who never had a chance to meet the uncle that child would have become.

Writing deeply about "memory moments" like these often leads to discoveries, not only about that time in your life, but also its meaning.

2. Now, *Show* Us That Moment

Write as if you are a camera and you are recording a movie. Get close up. Focus on place, image, action, the concrete intimate detail. This invites your reader to *experience*—not just read—the story.

Write deeply about a "memory moment." This often leads to discoveries not only about that time in your life, but also its meaning.

Let's look at that example about a day at the lake. Here's one version:

My father packed the car for our trip to the lake. We bought ice on the way, picnicked on the grass, played a lot in the water, then finally drove home. It was a good day.

Credit: *Griet Cornille.*

The writer wants to share a story about a favorite memory. However, the writing is a little flat. The writer tells us it was a good day, but we don't feel it, and we don't realize it's one of her favorite memories. It doesn't allow us to get a sense of the child the writer once was and hear her real voice. The writing "tells" rather than "shows."

Lucky for her nieces and nephews, the writer decided to rewrite her photo caption. Let's take a look:

Show the moment. Concrete details put us right into the story. This makes writing more satisfying to read *and* to write.

My father packed our blue '63 Buick with a Coleman cooler filled with hot dogs and my mom's homemade sauerkraut. It was Sunday morning and already 88 degrees. He said we'd get ice on the way.

The writer's starting to use concrete details. We know what kind of car, and we understand that this family is "all-American" (they eat hot-dogs!) and a little traditional (the mom makes her own sauerkraut!). We suspect they go to the lake fairly regularly (they bought a Coleman, a brand name—something that's not here today, gone tomorrow, so they can use it a lot!).

Can't you just feel a story coming on? (The father said they'd get ice on the way. But it's going to be a scorcher! Uh-oh: What if they forget to stop for ice? What's going to happen to the food in the cooler?)

Let's see what this writer does next:

My brothers, sisters, and I ran to the car and waited. It was so hot that we had to open the windows and even then sweat rolled down the middle of my back.

Our writer's on her way! She's beginning to show, not tell, her story.

Remember to do likewise when you write *your* story. Write it so that *your reader is right there in the story with you,* experiencing, as much as possible, the events you lived through, the emotions you felt. That kind of story is not only more satisfying to read, but a lot more satisfying to write.

3. Arrange the Moments (Scenes) in an Artful Way

Let's leave our writer alone to finish her story while we consider not just the *what* of the story but also the *how* and the *why* of it.

If you've ever struggled with telling a story, you might have gotten this advice: just start at the beginning, and tell what happened next. This is generally good advice.

But not all stories need to start at the beginning. Nor should stories explain too much or give too much background.

When we talk about telling your story "in an artful way," we mean find a "shape" or arrangement that fits your story and include only those details that support the memory you want to share and what's important about

Credit: Laura Musikanski.

Find a good "shape" for your story. You can "begin at the beginning," of course—or in any of several different ways. Find an arrangement that makes sense for the story you want to tell and that is easy for your readers to follow.

that memory. Though it often makes sense to tell a story in chronological order—maybe even (if it's a long story covering many years) using a diary style with dated entries that keep your reader on track with time and place—you could also arrange the events in your story by doing the following:

- Starting with the part of the story that has the most excitement or the most tension (lots of movies start this way), then circling back to the beginning and telling the story in chronological order until the end (*My brothers and I could hardly wait for my parents to finish packing the car. We were going to the lake for a full day of swimming!*)

- Starting with a remark someone made, then filling in the rest of the story through his/her eyes (movies that use "voiceover" narration do this) (*"It's so hot! Dad, can we go swimming at the lake today?" Swimming was my favorite thing in the whole world . . .*)

- Starting with the least important detail and then adding details in increasing order of importance (*When we got home from church, I helped my mother wrap hot dogs in foil. When we finished, she said, "Ask your dad to put these in the cooler."*)

- Starting to set the scene (*It was going to be a scorcher—the thermometer read 88 degrees—and the only thing my brothers and I wanted to do that day was to go swimming at the lake*), then telling the rest of what happened

- Starting by telling us why you're telling this particular story, then launching into the story itself (*My parents never understood why I hated sauerkraut, so I'm going to set the record straight. It all started when . . .*)

- Starting, as our writer decided to do, with letting us see what is happening and then dripping in details little by little to pull us along with her. Here's how she put it all together:

My father packed our blue '63 Buick with a Coleman cooler filled with hot dogs and my mom's homemade sauerkraut. It was Sunday morning and already 88 degrees. He said we'd get ice on the way. My brothers, sisters, and I ran to the car and waited. It was so hot that we had to open the windows and even then sweat rolled down the middle of my back. By the time we got to the ice machine I could already smell sauerkraut even before my Dad opened the cooler to pour in the ice. Whew! I made up my mind there and then never again to eat that stinky stringy trussed-up cabbage!

Sometimes these different arrangements will overlap. That's fine. The important thing is to use an arrangement that makes sense for the story you want to tell. Think in terms of pattern: what kind of pattern are you setting up that's *interesting* and *easy* for your readers to follow?

Then *Voila!* You've now got a story with impact, a story readers will remember, if not forever, for a really long time.

4. Treat Your Writing Like Play-Doh

One of the shelves in my bookcase holds some objects designed to inspire my writing. There's a book (*Women of Words*), a basket full of drawing pens in fun colors, a one-inch picture frame I found at a department store, a stone, and a jar of Play-Doh.

By now you know why the picture frame is there. How about the stone and the Play-Doh?

The stone reminds me to be free with my words. My words are not stone—immutable, unchangeable. Instead they are Play-Doh; they can be shaped many different ways to tell the story I want to tell. No matter how many words or how much effort it took to get those words out on paper, there's "always more where that came from." I should spend words freely—adding some here, taking away lots there—to tell the story the best way I know how.

Treat your writing like Play-Doh. Your words can be shaped in many ways. If you choose to revise, take it one step at a time, and don't be afraid to make changes.

Again, I take inspiration from Anne Lamott—I write a terrible first draft and get everything out of my head and onto the page. Then I go back and revise my story one step at a time. I ask myself questions like the following:

- What is this about? Does everything I've jotted down relate to the story I want to tell—or could it be taken out and saved for another story?
- Where can I add concrete details?
- Can I use these details in a way that makes readers feel as though they're right in the story with me?

- Where can I show more action?
- Where can I use dialogue?
- Is everything as emotionally true as I can make it?

Our diligent writer asked herself these questions, too, and then made a few more changes:

One Sunday, as soon as we got home from church, ~~Mm~~y father ~~packed~~ carried the Coleman cooler filled with hot dogs and my mom's home-made sauerkraut to the trunk of our blue '63 Buick ~~with a Coleman cooler filled with hot dogs and my mom's homemade sauerkraut~~. It was only 10 o'clock and ~~Sunday morning and~~ already 88 degrees. We were going to the lake! "We'll get ice on the way," my father said, and so ~~He said we'd get ice on the way.~~ ~~Mm~~y brothers~~, sisters,~~ and I ~~ran~~ raced to the car ~~and waited~~. What was taking my parents so long? It was so hot that we had to open the windows and even then sweat rolled down the middle of my back. ~~By the time~~ When we got to the ice machine I jumped out of the car to get some fresh air while my Dad popped open the trunk and got the ice. While I waited for him to return, I leaned into the trunk and lifted the cooler's lid. Ugh. That air wasn't fresh at all. In fact, it smelled like farts. ~~I could already smell sauerkraut even before my Dad opened the cooler to pour in the ice.~~ Whew! I made up my mind there and then never again to eat that stinky stringy trussed-up cabbage!

She reads it over, and feels happy about the changes she made. She reads it one more time—then decides to include a little humor at the end by adding this:

"That's all right," my Dad said. "More for us."

5. Believe in Even the Smallest Details of a Life, and in Your Own Voice

We connect through story, and story is made up of details, artfully rendered, in our own authentic voice.

Have faith in that voice. Be the most "you" you can be. There is only one you, and no one else has lived your life. And so,

Write your story as it needs to be written. Write it honestly, and tell it as best you can. I'm not sure that there are any other rules. Not ones that matter.

—Neil Gaiman

Keep in Mind

The techniques presented in this chapter are simple tips anyone can use to make a memoir memorable. To review, here are the five steps:

1. Choose a moment.
2. *Show* that moment.
3. Arrange the moments in an artful way.
4. Treat your writing like Play-Doh.
5. Trust the details and trust your voice.

If writing your memoir energizes you and you find yourself wanting to delve even more deeply into writing, we recommend Ralph Fletcher's *How to Write Your Life Story* (Collins, 2007).

And please remember that even though this chapter is about "crafting" your story, often the original draft comes out whole and shouldn't be tinkered with. Learn to recognize the difference.

How *do* you recognize that difference, you ask? Especially if you're new to writing?

Read what you've written aloud to someone who doesn't know your story, then ask the person to tell it back to you. If she "got" what you wanted to

Credit: *MorgueFile.com.*

Make your memoir "memorable." Sometimes a story comes out whole, and sometimes it needs more work to make it memorable. How do you tell the difference? Read it aloud to someone. If she "gets it" then you know your work is done.

come across, if she wasn't confused about anything, if she laughed or drew in a breath at the right places, if she smiled or sighed in recognition—that's how you know your work is done.

FAQs: Overcoming Common Stumbling Blocks

Deciding to write your story could bring up some perplexing questions. Here are some that we often hear—and our responses.

Q: I'm really not very good at writing. My English teacher used to redline all of my compositions! But my children are asking me to put my life stories down on paper. Help!?

A: Check out "Getting Over Your Fear of Writing" in the Appendix section of this book. It will boost your confidence, give you lots of ideas for getting started, and help you overcome any obstacles (like the memory of that critical English teacher!).

Q: As I'm writing, I'm finding the need to fill in some holes—like the historical context of my life's events. How do I do this?

A: Let's go from simple ideas to more complex ones:

- Brainstorm a list of expressions the people in your life used, like "holy smokes" or "the bees' knees" and use them in description or dialogue.

- Mention toys, songs, television shows, cars, etc., that were typical of the times.

- Interview the people you are writing about for information on things you might not have known or remembered as a child.
- Include stories about the places you spent time, for example, the annual holiday party at the Polish National Home, or the Girls and Boys Club.
- Research the newspapers of that era for newsworthy events to include. The Newseum in Washington, D.C., for instance, archives the front pages of many world newspapers (www.newseum.org/todaysfront-pages). Your local librarian can help you find local newspapers. For more extensive research, consider the National Archives (archives. gov/research), which catalogs information on people (including military service records), places, and events.

Q: I'm worried about spilling family secrets or offending someone I write about if I tell a true story about my family or my life. What should I do?

A: Every writer approaches that differently. Here are some approaches writers we know have taken:

- "It's my life, and I'm entitled to my story."
- "It's my life, but I'd like you to read the parts that concern you to see if that's how you remember it, or if you have any perspectives you think I should add." Keep in mind that if the person objects, you then have a choice: heed their objections and take out the offending material or decide to keep your story as it is.
- "I'm going to wait until the person I am writing about is dead."
- "I'm going to tell my story, but only the positive parts."

- "I'm going to tell my story, but put a disclaimer at the beginning that lets people know this is how I saw things, and others may have different views."

- "I'm going to write the story, change the names and identifying details, and call it a novel."

Q: The memoir I want to write is not the story of my life, but the story of someone important in my family history who's still alive. Where do I start?

A: Lucky you! You can start by interviewing the person (see chapter 7 for tips) and/or people who know that person. Assuming the person feels comfortable with you writing his or her story, ask if he or she can share letters, photo albums, or any other artifacts that might be useful in pulling together the information you'll need. For example, author Debbie Levy used her mother's autograph book as the starting point for writing about her mother's escape from Berlin in World War II.

You might find it easiest to start by deciding on a theme or focus for the story, for example, the relative's role in the Army, the person's career as a minister, your relative's adventures sailing around the world— whatever the two of you decide would make the most sense.

Q: What if the person I want to write about isn't living anymore?

A: That's a little trickier. But here are some ideas for where to start:

- Your memories of the person and your life with him or her.

- Interviews with people who knew the person you are writing about.

- Heirlooms or any family records or artifacts, including letters, scrapbooks, etc., that might provide insights into the person's character or lifestyle.
- Genealogical research, to fill in any gaps in history that you want to include. Here are some sources:
  o Ellis Island (www.ellisisland.org) for information on immigrants that arrived via Atlantic passage
  o Ancestry.com (www.ancestry.com) or "101 Ways to Research Your Family Tree for Free" (http://genealogy.about.com/cs/free_genealogy/a/free_sites.htm) for genealogy records
  o Each state and county has civil records like birth certificates, marriage licenses, divorce records, etc.
  o Churches also keep records of marriages, baptisms, etc. (see chapter 8, "You Are the Bridge").

Again, you might find it easier (and more interesting for your readers) to begin writing if you decide on a focus or take a "slice of life" approach to telling that person's story.

Q: How do I incorporate facts—or other description, for that matter—without being boring?

A: Bestselling author Marcy Heidish believes in using "the I.V. drip method." In other words, incorporate facts a little at a time. Bring in the relevant details *as your reader needs to know them,* rather than chunking them all into one paragraph (called an "info dump"). It makes for more interesting storytelling.

Q: I want to use dialogue to make the people I'm writing about come alive, but I can't remember the exact words they used. How do I deal with this?

A: Memory is indeed fickle, but that's no reason to completely leave out dialogue. When recounting events, include your best memory of what happened and what was said—just enough to keep the story line going. There's no need to include an entire conversation. You're after emotional truth. Your goal in including dialogue is to include dialogue that advances your story, reveals character personality, and lets the reader feel like he's eavesdropping!

You saw one example of this in the story about going to swim at the lake. Here's another:

My grandpa was a quiet man so I don't remember his saying much, but I remember after supper his telling my frugal grandma, "A second cookie isn't going to spoil the child." I always knew he was in my corner.

Q: How do I edit my work so that it's more interesting to my readers?

A: Rewriting and editing definitely refine and improve a story. Here's how to do it:

- First, let your draft sit for a while (a few days or weeks) before making any judgments about it.

- When you're ready to work with it again and can give it a fresh ear and eye, explore one or more of these "feedback" mechanisms:

o Ask yourself what you wanted to show in the piece . . . and what you want your reader to get. If that isn't happening, then work on making it so.

o Read it silently. Note the places you want to skip over; they are probably nonessential, or need to be worked into the story or recounted in more interesting ways. Note the places you "lean into"; they are the interesting or "juicy" parts and should stay.

o Read the piece out loud to yourself. The places you stumble over need some work.

o Remember the earlier suggestion about reading the piece out loud to somebody else (or to a whole group of somebody elses)? You'll be able to tell the places that connect because your listeners will make audible sounds. Pieces that connect emotionally with readers connect with the body—readers react viscerally. They might gasp, laugh, sigh, or give that final grunt that means "wow."

o Share the piece with a reader you trust—generally not a family member, by the way. Ask the reader to tell you what she understood to be happening, what she learned from the story, and what questions she had or what she wondered about. Those answers will clue you into whether your piece is doing what you wanted it to do.

Q: I'm writing my life, so what's wrong with letting people make of it what they will instead of spending time rewriting and editing my work?

A: Writing for yourself is fine. That's the healing aspect of crafting your story—getting your stories "off your back" and onto the page. If you're writing for readers, however, you have a different goal: reaching and touching your readers with your story. If that's your goal, write it so that readers *want* to read what you have to say.

Chapter 3
AROUND THE TABLE: FOOD AND COOKBOOK MEMOIRS

— By Dianne Hennessy King —

There are so many reasons to create a food memoir: as a family legacy, as a bridal or graduation gift, as a remembrance of your travels, or as a record of entertaining friends and family in your own home. You already have the creativity and motivation, now you just need a little know-how.

Whether you have a half-dozen recipes or a shoebox full of notes, newspaper clippings, and scribbled cards handed down from your family, you can create a food memoir that tells the stories of who you are, what meals you shared at the kitchen table, when and where you lived, and how you celebrated special events.

You might be wondering what a food memoir is. Usually it has more of a theme, more personal stories, and more of the personality of the person or persons creating it than a traditional cookbook. It can be a slice of life of a certain time or place, like your summer vacations as a kid visiting your grandparents in Mississippi, or the summer vacation you are planning for this year. Maybe you're looking back on your first year of cooking on your own or forward to making cookies with your kids. Whoever you are, whatever your reasons, and whatever form you choose, *your* voice should be the one the reader or listener hears.

Credit: *Dianne Hennessy King.*

Recipe collection. Begin your memoir by gathering your recipe notes, clippings, emails, and stories.

Granted, a lot of famous people like Julia Child or former *Gourmet* editor-in-chief Ruth Reichl write bestselling food memoirs. You also see reviews of books by people going off to France, Timbuktu, or wherever to answer their life's questions while learning how to make the perfect loaf of bread, but that's probably not the case for most of us. More of us are like my student, Janice. She wanted to remember her grandmother Maude and Maude's life during the Depression and war years in the same region depicted in the television program *The Waltons*, written by Earl Hamner, Jr. Another student, Lydia, put together a notebook of favorite foods for her thirty-year-old daughter to keep alive the stories of Lydia and her Ukrainian family's emigration to northern Minnesota from a refugee camp after World War II. We want to share our recipes, but we also want to tell what the foods mean to us. Who made it for us, where were we, why do we want to tell about it? Memoir/Memories. There's a reason those words are so connected.

In this chapter you will find a list of ten questions to jog memories of shared meals, tips on food photography made easy, and guidelines for recipe writing and clear layouts. *All of that information will help you no matter what type of food memoir project you pick.* You will learn how you can create your food memoir as a cookbook, an essay, a cooking video, a CD, a quilt, an oral history, or a blog. Included are photos of *homemade* memoir cookbooks and examples of ways to personalize your food memoir with family stories, maps, documents, photos and more.

Find Your Memories: Ten Questions That Will Trigger Your Memories (and Your Taste Buds)

We all eat meals every day, and yet we can be stumped when someone asks us what we ate last week or when we were a child. This list of ten questions will help you start remembering.

1. **What is your earliest memory of food? Do you remember where you lived at the time?**

   Was it Halloween candy in a sack or your big brother pouring cereal? French fries at the beach or your mom feeding you warm rice? It can take some time to think back to when you were little. Don't forget to also ask your family and friends what their earliest memories are to jog your own memory and theirs.

2. **What did you usually eat for breakfast? For lunch?**

   Did you eat breakfast in the kitchen? Who else was at the table with you? What did you see when you looked out the window—apartment buildings, trees, a road? Did you have a favorite food that went into your lunchbox, and was Roy Rogers or Star Wars on the cover? Or did you walk home for lunch, or buy school lunches?

3. **Did you absolutely hate any foods as a child? Did you *have* to eat them? Did you later change your mind about any of the foods?**

   So many of us have memories of hating something like peas or broccoli as a child and having to sit at the table until they were eaten. *Ugh.*

Are you surprised that some of those foods taste good to you now? Or are you unrepentant in your dislike of peas?

4. **Can you remember a "first time" for tasting a specific food or dish that seemed exotic or strange to you?**

Think about how it felt on the tongue, whether or not you liked it, and who gave it to you. Was it an avocado, sushi, or a margarita? You might have been someplace different (on a vacation or visiting relatives in Kansas), but it also might have been food from the next-door neighbors.

5. **Do you connect certain foods with certain people in your childhood?**

For someone, it is homemade bread baked with a grandmother; for another whose father traveled a lot, it was the barbecue chicken his dad made when he was home.

6. **Do you associate certain foods with particular civic or national holidays like Independence Day, New Year's Day, Memorial Day, or Labor Day?**

I had hot dogs and hamburgers every Fourth of July—did you? Were you always at a picnic on Memorial or Labor Day? Instead of January 1st, maybe your New Year's Day followed a lunar calendar like Chinese and Persian celebrations.

7. **Are there any foods you connect with religious or cultural holidays?**

Was it turkey or lasagna for Thanksgiving, and was the salad always lime Jell-O? Hanukkah, Christmas, Diwali? Were special foods served for a Bar Mitzvah or Quinceañera celebration? Or fusion foods like green bagels for St. Patrick's Day?

8. **Did your family have any food preferences for family celebrations?**

    Maybe a child got to pick out the menu for his or her birthday meal or eat take-out every other day when on vacation? First day of spring picnic? Special desserts for good grades on Report Card Day?

9. **What was your greatest comfort with routine?**

    For example, "On Sunday, we always had . . .?" What was your greatest enjoyment in breaking a routine, like eating *dessert* before dinner?

10. **Did your family use any particular foods or drinks for when people weren't feeling well? Any foods or drinks that were meant to help keep you healthy and strong?**

    Giving good food has always been a way we take care of ourselves and our loved ones. We all have our favorite cures for colds, such as garlic or lemons, special herbs, and chicken soup. What are your family's favorite foods to keep you well or to help when you're feeling sick?

Find Your Own Voice

After you have gathered a whole lot of memories by asking those ten questions, you are in a better position to start telling your stories. One thing to remember about writing a food memoir, as with all memoirs, is the importance of trusting your own voice. Your book or article or video doesn't need to sound like anyone else and, in fact, you don't *want* it to sound like anyone else.

Just to show you that no two voices or experiences are alike, here are a couple of stories from two of my students, both of them talking about a recipe for molasses cookies, both trying to capture the voices and charms of childhood.

Credit: Dianne Hennessy King.

Two stories of childhood molasses cookies show that no two voices or experiences are alike.

The first is a story from a wonderful newspaper reporter, Jane, who took my cookbook writing class and who delighted us all with her infectious sense of humor. Her son Jon loved her homemade pizza and molasses cookies when he was young. To accompany Jane's recipe for molasses cookies, she gave us a little background.

The story behind the molasses cookies is two-fold: Jon at two could not say molasses and called them "moss cookies." And, he was quite taken with the picture of the rabbit on the molasses jar label. When we lived in Colorado, we spent many a snowy afternoon baking cookies.

The second and longer story about molasses cookies was by another mother looking back at her childhood. She, too, tells her story in her own wonderful way. This story accompanied Mary's family recipe for molasses cookies.

When I was a very little girl (maybe four years old), I was taken by my grandparents to their church picnic. I did not know anyone there other than my grandparents, and I was the only child present. After dinner, the men and women separated into two groups, and I went with the ladies group to something called a "prayer circle." There must have been thirty women and me in this group.

I didn't know what a "prayer circle" was, but I soon learned that we all were to hold hands, sit in a large circle, and each person had to say something for which she was grateful. I could think of a few things I was grateful for (my family, my friends, my pets), but they got used up by the first several ladies, and Grandma and I were almost at the end of the circle. I was only four, and I was really scared, because I didn't want to embarrass my grandmother by admitting that I was clean out of gratitude. Four-year-olds can't always come up with world peace, freedom from tyranny, beauty, truth, justice, etc.—especially on such short notice. Most of these women had seventy or eighty years of things to be grateful for, and I felt very disadvantaged.

I knew that if I didn't say something really acceptable, my mother and father would be disappointed in me, and the rest of my life would probably be filled with lectures on what an ungrateful and undeserving person I was. Several of my relatives were already way too good at those lectures, and I just hated to give them more ammunition. The circle kept moving, and people were grateful for the nice weather, for birds, and trees, and gardens, and for the opportunity to be together (which, as you might imagine, was not high on my list at the time). Nothing was inspiring me. I thought about running away, but knew I'd eventually have to return. There was no getting out of it. There was not a darned thing I could think of that made me grateful.

Then, when it was my turn, I blurted out that I was grateful that my Grandma had brought such good molasses cookies. The ladies liked it. I was saved by divine inspiration. I have always been grateful for these cookies.

If you can talk about it, you can write about it, the same as if you were telling a friend.

Show Us the Food

When writing your food memoir, consider using photos to "show" as well as "tell" your story. Here are some ways to use photos in your food memoir.

Cover Photo

What's your food memoir going to be about? Is it the story of your family history, or is it a collection of friends' recipes for a bride and groom, or will the book be a fundraiser for your favorite cause? Choose a cover photo to reflect that idea.

This photo is of a painting by a grandmother that shows her teaching her granddaughter how to make tortillas. Grandma's guiding hands are passing

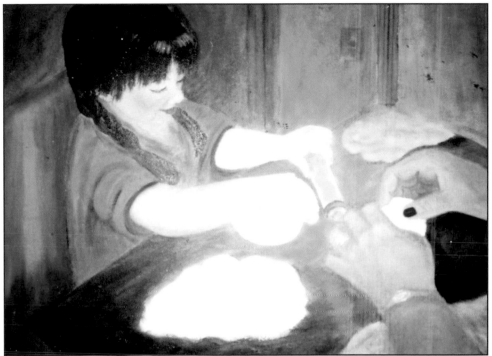

Credit: Dianne Hennessy King.

Use images to show and tell your story. A grandmother painted this picture in which she is teaching her granddaughter the traditional way to make tortillas.

on her experience and history to the future generation. We put this image on the cover of a class cookbook called *Cooking from Memories*. Cover photos aren't just for books; they can be used as the opening page of a calendar, a CD, or any other memoir format you choose.

Sometimes you want to simply give the mood of a time and place to the beginning of your project. This photo of cherry blossoms blooming in April adorned the cover of a handmade cookbook from a springtime class in Washington,

Credit: Dianne Hennessy King.

Give a sense of a time and place. Cherry blossoms are blooming on the cover of a handmade cookbook from a springtime class in Washington, D.C.

D.C. The blossoms indicate the time and the Washington Monument in the background of the photo tell you the setting.

You might want a book cover that conveys a more modern tone, because the beautiful food is being shown in a fresh way in an unusual setting.

Credit: *Dianne Hennessy King.*

Show food in an eye-catching way. This cookbook cover features an apple cake shown outdoors.

This apple cake is shown outdoors and the soft, delicate cake is in contrast to the beautiful white stone boulder. The photo is also more attention-getting because the food is not directly in the center of the scene.

You Can Do It Yourself

Every food memoir needs lots of good pictures that make you want to jump in and start cooking. Take a look at your favorite cookbooks and magazines to see how the photography was done. But here's the good news—you can do it yourself! You don't need a professional test kitchen or studio set-up to capture some beautiful shots for your own food project.

Photography Tips

These tips will help you get professional-looking results.

- **Shoot photos *outdoors*** or with daylight coming through a window. If you need just a touch of extra light, place something white—a white napkin or teapot—next to the part of the close-up scene that is in a shadow and the white will help bounce up the light. Keep an eye on the background in order to include flowers, landscapes, tabletops, people, or whatever helps tell your story.

- **Take lots of pictures!** Especially with digital cameras and mobile phone cameras, there's no extra cost for film, so keep snapping the shutter. Check out smartphone apps that can transform your photos. For example, an app called Waterlogue can turn your realistic photo into a watercolor painting. My advice to all food photographers would be an echo of Julia Child's direction to cooks reading her memoir: *"This is my invariable advice to people: Learn how to cook—try new recipes, learn from your mistakes, be fearless, and above all, **have fun**."* Substitute "take photos" for "cook" and "photos" for "recipes," and that about sums it all up.

- **Shoot from *above*.** Carefully stand on a step stool to shoot the photo, although you can also get good close-ups from above when you are standing on the floor or ground.

Credit: *Dianne Hennessy King.*

Choose meaningful objects to photograph with the food. This fire hydrant and china dog reinforce the distinctiveness of healthy, homemade dog biscuits made in the shape of a fire hydrant.

45

- **Shoot from the *side.*** Take shots two, three, and four feet away from the food. Also, try shooting with unusual objects surrounding the food so you can tell a story. The photo of the dog biscuits is for a homemade and healthy pet food booklet inspired by a pet owner's efforts to nurse her dog back to health.

Credit: *Dianne Hennessy King.*

Show the steps. How-to photos show bread dough in three stages. Yeast proofing. First rise with thumb indentation. Second rise; ready to bake.

- **Shoot a series** of how-to photos to explain a cooking technique like making a sauce, such as hollandaise or hot fudge, or a dough for cinnamon rolls. It is helpful to have step-by-step photos (or drawings) for any recipe where the changes in shape or color of the ingredients tell you whether you're making the recipe correctly—or not.

- **Take photos in black-and-white as well as color.** Using a black-and-white or sepia version of your ingredients can give the recipe a feeling of going back in time, in addition to showing the beauty of the food. Adjustments to color filters can also give photos a "retro" look.

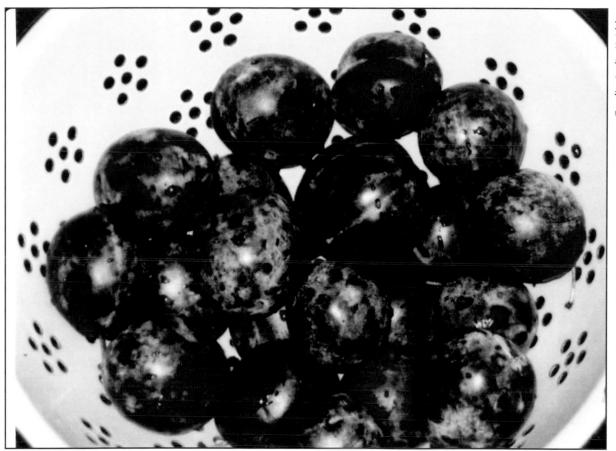

Credit: *Judie Keithley.*

Purple plums. Take photos of ingredients before and after they are used in a recipe.

Plum cake.

- **Before and after.** Take photos of ingredients like these purple plums before they are baked into a German Plum Cake. This is one of the easiest ways to let the beauty of food just shine.

Other Illustrations

Add old magazine or advertising illustrations that are from a similar time to one of your collected recipes. If you save an illustration from the internet, make sure it's in the public domain with no copyright. The good news is that most

Credit: *Library of Congress.*

Add old magazine or advertising illustrations. Use images that are in the public domain and relevant to the recipe, story, or time period.

graphics and old maps and historical advertisements *are* in the public domain. The online photography and old-time graphics collection at the Library of Congress (www.loc.gov) is one of several excellent resources. See the Appendix for more.

To give your food stories a sense of time, place, and background, you can include not just food photos and family photos, but also hometown maps, family trees, and scanned documents like a birth certificate or the deed to the family farm. Online newspaper archives are a terrific source for headlines and articles about your history.

When you use an image from the internet, make sure to save the highest quality version you can find. Download files from the source, like the Library of Congress, instead of right-clicking and copying from a simple web search. This will make your images crisp and clear when you print out your memoir.

How to Write a Recipe

Now that you have your stories and your graphics, how do you explain to someone how he or she can actually make this food that means so much to you? Well, recipes can be written in many different ways. Take a look at some of your favorite cookbooks or food blogs and try to figure out what appeals to you. No matter which layout pattern you choose, here are some basic guidelines to follow:

- Introductory description—can include origin of recipe (relative, book, friend)
- Preparation time, cooking time, number of servings
- Ingredients list
- Step-by-step method for chopping, mixing, etc.
- Family story connected to recipe: you fixed it for your brother's thirtieth birthday, or you always had it at a favorite restaurant on summer vacation at your grandparents' house
- A photo, if possible, of either the food itself or a gathering or occasion when the food might have been served

Putting Your Collection Together in Print

Here are some page layout basics to give your cookbook a professional look.

Font

Font is the print style of the letters of the alphabet. You've probably noticed these styles in the "formatting ribbon" that is part of a word processing program—you'll see names like "Book Antiqua" or "Times New Roman" or "Helvetica," for example.

Plain print that is clear and not squiggly helps cooks who are busy in the kitchen! Most importantly, choose a font style that pleases you and helps the reader clearly understand your recipes and stories. Nowadays, there are so many beautiful fonts that will help you create a unique project that reflects your personality and voice.

Font Color

While we're talking about font, pay attention to the color of the letters and the color of the background. In recent years, the art departments of magazines and books have gone a little color crazy. Have you struggled to read ingredients written in "sunshine" yellow placed against an "eggplant" background? White or grey letters on a black background? It may look artistic, but it is just making life harder for the cook. Please, put yourself in your reader's shoes before you pick out styles, sizes, and colors.

Font Size

Recipe titles should be a little bit bigger than the text and list of ingredients. A two-point spread is good, but you can make the difference larger if you wish. For example, you could set the title in 13 point and the main recipe in 11 point font. Other examples: 16 or 18 point (title)/10 or 12 point (list of ingredients). Whatever you choose, keep it consistent.

Headnotes and Sidebars

You might want to use one or both of these to convey additional information about either the specific recipe or the theme of the book. You can use different type treatments such as *italic* or **bold** to create a consistently identifiable thread throughout the book. The HEADNOTE can offer all kinds of information, from oddities of ingredients and shopping or serving advice to recipe history or background or a simple description of how the finished dish looks or tastes. The SIDEBAR (often in the shape of a box) can offer information on anything from the fishermen of Savannah to the history of basil in Italian cooking, depending on the theme and layout of your book. SIDEBARS do not have to be on the side of the page.

Columns

Choose a one- or two-column format for the ingredient list. You may want to do a trial format of both methods for one whole chapter before you make your final decision. You can waste a lot of space with a one-column list, but if you want a good amount of white space on a page and you want no confusion with the ingredients, you might want to choose the single column. However, you can conserve space by using two columns, and you might want to use the two-column format if your book will be wider than tall.

Page Layout

Decide on the margin size. Decide left or right justification (alignment) of text. Decide portrait (tall) or landscape (wide) orientation; that decision often depends on the final page size you have selected for the book.

Headers and Footers

Decide where your page breaks will go. Do you want the book title on top of every page, or only on each right-hand page? Decide if you want a chapter title on every page or perhaps only on the left- or right-hand pages, or not at all. Decide if you want the recipe title at the top of each page in addition to placing it above the list of ingredients. Decide if your page number is to be at the center bottom of the page or at the corner bottom, top center, or corner top (your word processing program will give you options in the header and footer menu).

Example of a Page Layout

Let's imagine the following recipe has been included in a book called *Home Cooking*. The book title is flush left on each page; the chapter title and page number are flush right; the headnote is in italics below the recipe title; font is Book Antiqua, size 10 and the recipe title is size 14, centered, ingredients size 11, in a single column, flush left. Method is written in narrative style rather than Steps 1, 2, 3 . . . .

If you arrange the ingredients in a two-column layout, any photos or sidebars would likely be at top or bottom of page or on the facing page. If you arrange the ingredients in a one-column layout as shown here, you could have space to put photos or sidebars to the side of the ingredients. Also, in a one-column layout, you have room to spell out tablespoon and teaspoon. In the old days, one often omitted serving numbers for familiar foods such as a pie. You can always add servings and directions that weren't present in the original recipes but that might be useful to modern cooks, such as "Serves 6–8" and "Mix all ingredients together and pour into an unbaked pie shell."

Home Cooking   *Pies Page 43*

Sarah Walker Mercer's

Sweet Potato Pie

Sarah Walker Mercer was a custodian at Louise Archer Elementary School in Vienna, Virginia. Mrs. Mercer was a beloved member of the entire community and a mentor, confidante, and supporter of children and teachers. A park that is close to the school is named in her honor. One day, years ago, when Nadine James ("Nurturing the Young Storyteller") was a teacher at Louise Archer, the school was going to celebrate Louise Archer Day. Nadine said, "I was unsure of what to bring to the soul food luncheon, and Sarah wrote down this recipe for me. I baked her sweet potato pie for the event, and I have been sharing it with my family and friends ever since. When she passed away years later, I still was using her original handwritten recipe as my guide."

Ingredients:

1½ cups mashed sweet potatoes

½ cup sugar

1 teaspoon cinnamon

1 teaspoon allspice

½ teaspoon salt

3 eggs

1 cup milk

2 Tablespoons butter, melted

Credit: Dianne Hennessy King.

Layouts of recipes and photos. Place a food photo above, to the side, below, or with text wrapped around the recipe in a page layout.

Method: Bake at 350° for 40–50 minutes.

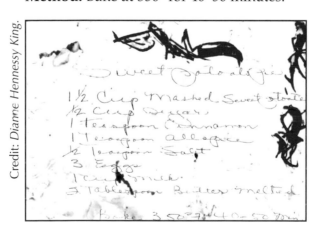

Credit: Dianne Hennessy King.

Add personal touches, such as a story about when the dish was served or a handwritten copy of the recipe.

Food Memoir Your Way

Now that you know what a food memoir is, how to decide on a theme and find your voice, how to take photos and find graphics, and how to write a recipe that works, let's have even more fun in creating a *Memoir Your Way*. Choose a way that appeals to you.

Make an Oral History Around Food That Links Family Generations Together

If you want to choose a family project, you might want to start with taking a closer look at the "Find Your Memories: Ten Questions That Will Trigger Your Memories (and Your Taste Buds)." These are questions to ask yourself, but they are also great questions for a child to ask her grandparents, aunts, and uncles. Sometimes grandparents become shy or hesitant when asked questions such as "What was it like way back then?" The Greatest Generation doesn't tend to talk about themselves. I can guarantee you, though, that asking "What was your favorite food?" will get the conversation started, and one memory leads to another. You can write down some oral histories but you can also just do an audio recording via any sort of a tape recorder. See chapter 7, "Nurturing the Young Storyteller," for some more techniques.

You don't have to skip a generation for the food questions to be helpful. One of my students said she had known her mother-in-law for twenty years, but it wasn't until she had asked her the ten food memory questions that she learned so much more about her husband's family history. Food can be a comforting, familiar subject, and once you begin to talk about it, so many connecting stories appear. Who helped with the harvest, what did the home country's bread taste like, how did we make do when times were hard or celebrate when times were good?

Videotape Your Own Food Network

Think how great it would be to see and hear your brother tell you how he makes his barbecue—mixing up the sauce or spice rub, lighting the grill, setting up the direct and indirect heat and maybe the wood chips, what the food looks like just at the perfect point before you flip it to the other side. It feels as if you're standing right beside him, taking in all his secrets, and once you've taped it, you have his voice, smile, and advice forever.

Maybe it's your best friend who's a whiz at making bread. You know you have followed the exact same recipe that she uses, and yet your bread never tastes as good as hers. Go ahead and videotape the key steps, using a camera or a smartphone or tablet. What does proofed yeast look like, anyway? Flat? Furry? Fuzzy? Jumping around? Does she rotate the dough every time she kneads the dough towards her and then away? If she sticks her fingertips in the dough to test if it has risen enough, what do the holes in the dough look like? What does "hollow" sound like if she thumps each loaf of bread in the oven to hear if it's cooked enough? Have her tell you how she learned to make bread and record your laughs about how you've each baked a few bricks of fallen dough. Whether you're capturing on video someone making bread or making barbecue, all that's missing are the great smells.

Create CDs for Special Occasions

These are great for bridal and baby showers, graduations, birthdays, community groups, travelogues, and personal mementos. When you want a written record from a community—you ask all the people invited to a gathering to contribute recipes and photos for the guest of honor—simply scan their material into your computer (if they have sent it to you by snail mail) and create a CD. If the friends or family of the mother-to-be (for example) are scattered all over the country and are somewhat computer savvy, they can easily send you their recipes, photos, and stories online to collect into the gift CD. Once you create a file for the CD, you can then send the file online to anyone, anywhere. No books to ship and no delivery delays. Remember, a written record doesn't necessarily mean a printed-out record.

For community groups such as schools or churches, you can make a CD of recipes and photos of bake sales and use the CD as an additional fundraiser. It is easy to take a photo of each of the foods before the bake sale begins. Have each donor either scan her own recipe and send it to you, or the donor can write out his recipe and then you can scan it and match all the recipes with the matching photos. Just like that, you have a recipe collection created in one day. Take orders for the recipe collection CD file at the bake sale and you won't even have to do any follow-up sales!

Write a Book, a Booklet, or an Article

You would be surprised at how many books started with someone simply writing a short article for a school project or a newsletter or as genealogy research. Earlier I mentioned my student Janice who wanted to write about her grandmother Maude and her recipes. When she started my class, she had already gathered a sheaf of recipes and photos, but she gradually came to see that if she told the fuller story of Maude's life and times, it would be even more interesting. The point is to *start* where you are—you can always add to the basic story later as you find out more. Janice went on to add all sorts of fun information, such as the fact that Albemarle Pippin apples from rural Virginia were a favorite at Queen Victoria's table. Who knew?

You might also prefer to start by writing a short article, for example, about the history of a traditional family recipe. Where did it come from and how did it change over geography and time? For example, did the recipe for spaghetti sauce originate in Sicily with homegrown tomatoes and lots of fresh herbs? When the family moved to Detroit, how did it change to accommodate American life in terms of taste, available ingredients, and available free time?

And then, there are always books. Food memoirs can be centered on one person, one or many families, or community-based memoirs. You can have ten recipes or five hundred. One of my students, along with a few friends, created a fundraising book to help pay for the church choir to travel to Italy. If you set up a template for a recipe layout (see sample layout on pages 54–55), you can have each contributor give a recipe in exactly the same format, which makes coordination a lot simpler. If you are working with a smaller group of contributors, let's say under a dozen, you could set up a Google Drive or other collaborative online document so that you could all work on the same food memoir and keep track of any changes any of you make.

However, when you are the only author, you get to make all the decisions. And that's how a majority of food memoirs are made.

Quilt a Food Memoir

A cookbook might be the first thing we think of as a food memoir, but it isn't the only way to go. Take a look at the quilting chapter for inspiration for beginners, and then turn a favorite recipe into a quilt design. For example, you could make a recipe-inspired appliqué that would transform your favorite recipe into a small art quilt that could be a great wall hanging, framed exhibit, or the center of a table runner.

Cut shapes of simplified recipe ingredients using interesting fabrics and stitch the shapes onto a background fabric. You might choose a shaft of wheat, a basket of red apples, a stick of yellow butter, and a rolling pin as the partners for a cut-out shape of your best apple pie in your favorite pie pan. Who knew that quilts could be mouth-watering? Every time you look at your quilt on the wall or on the table, you'll be reminded of all the times you made your apple pie for friends and family.

Photo Storybooks

Printed and online photo books are often created as travel mementos. When you travel, the food of a region or country is always tied up with the history of a place and is a reflection of the daily lives of the people of that region or country. There has been a nice expansion of format options on offer in just the last few years. Before, the templates were narrowly set and you couldn't add much more than a caption to the photo or a paragraph of description. In new books, you can add just about any written material that you want. Plan one of these photo books now, *before* your next trip, and you'll have much more fun eating your way through the cities and back roads of wherever you travel.

Create a Food Blog

Food blogs barely existed ten years ago; now there are thousands upon thousands of them. It is such a fast-growing form of communication, because blogs can be so immediate, personal, interactive, inexpensive, and completely independent of geography. You can find a way to blog almost anywhere you might live.

If you are unfamiliar with blogs, type "Top 100 Food Blogs" into your search engine and start reading. If you are already a visitor to a number of the more popular food blogs like *The Pioneer Woman,* you could check out PBS's list, "Ten Blogs You Should Be Reading, But Might Not Know About" as well as nominees and winners of *Saveur*'s blog awards. The writing is almost always less formal than in memoir books and more spontaneous because blog posts are often "posted" every day and are usually very reflective of the author. Go to a site like wordpress.com or blogspot.com, set up your own blog, and start writing. Everything you learned in this chapter about memories, voice, photography, and recipe-writing will help you create a livelier, more informative, and eye-catching blog.

Keep in Mind

- Choose a photo for the cover that shows the theme of the cookbook and/ or sets the time and place.

- Use questions to bring out details in your food memories. Remember that your food memoir doesn't have to sound like anyone else's, so trust your voice.

- If you are creating a printed food memoir, follow a consistent format in writing recipes and choosing fonts and page layouts to give it a professional look. Include lots of photographs and other graphics to make it inviting.

- Remember that your food memoir doesn't always have to be a book or something that's printed on paper. You can use your smartphone or your digital camera to create short cooking videos that you can download. Create a CD, record your child or grandparents talking about favorite foods, or make a simple quilt or a scrapbook for yourself. Whether you create a food memoir as a book, article, quilt, scrapbook, or video, it can all be easily shared online with family and friends.

- Food is love. It's as simple as that. Whatever way you choose to share that love and however you create your food memoir, you will have accomplished something wonderful, lasting, generous, and true.

Chapter 4
REINVENT YOUR SCRAPBOOK

—— By Katherine Nutt ——

Would you rather make something than write something? Are you better with your hands than with words? If so, apply your creative talents to making a scrapbook memoir—a new twist on a traditional scrapbook that combines visual appeal with storytelling.

A scrapbook is all about capturing life events, big and small, and that makes it a memoir. Maybe you already enjoy scrapbooking and are looking for new ideas. Or you'd like to put a story into words, but the thought of churning out pages of text is intimidating. You might be a more visual than verbal thinker, so transferring your thoughts into words seems difficult.

"Scrapping" your memoir might be the perfect way to both show and tell your stories. They might be the funny things your children said or the sad, traumatic, or even mundane events that helped shape the person you are. Write a little or a lot. Use a computer or a traditional paper-and-glue approach, or both. Tuck what you write into folds and under flaps, showcase it on pop-ups and pull-outs, or hide it away in pockets. This chapter suggests ways to use your creativity to produce a scrapbook memoir that will be as enjoyable for you to make as for others to view and read.

Beyond Captions

How much you write or journal in your scrapbook is up to you. But the more you write, the more meaning and charm your scrapbook will hold. Captions such as "Here's Dennis on his 5th birthday" leave much unsaid. Writing more will help you capture and preserve your stories in more depth and detail. Not only will your scrapbook be of more interest to others— because you'll be sharing more of your own personality and the personalities of those you write about—but you'll gain a better understanding of the events, people, and places in your life as you write about them. Here are some ways to start the stories flowing:

- Imagine yourself showing a scrapbook page or photo to a friend or relative. What would you say as you explain it? What is the story behind the picture that wouldn't come across if you didn't tell it?

- What was going on behind the scenes of a particular shot, or what happened before or after the captured moment? There you are on your first day of school or camp, your face lit with anticipation. Did it turn out the way you expected?

- In another photo your front teeth are missing. Why not write about the time your playmate Marsha knocked them out for you—by running at you with her fist—because you said you wished your teeth would fall out like everyone else's?

- If the photos are of a holiday or other special event, what were some of your favorite traditions? What delicious dish is making your mouth water as you pause to smile at the camera?

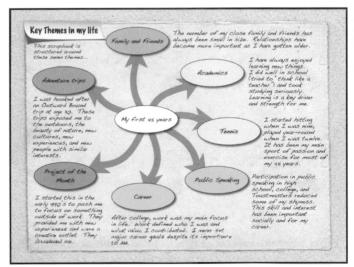

SCRAPBOOK PAGE BY *Daniel Sklar.*

Key themes. Management Consultant Daniel Sklar of Georgia made a scrapbook of the first forty-five years of his life. He began by summarizing his life's key themes and presenting them visually in a graphic.

- Consider the themes that would help you organize your scrapbook—achievements, vacations, places, and people—and the stories they bring to mind. For example, in a spread about "The House on Lincoln Avenue," you could write about the neighborhood games of kickball, kick-the-can, and marbles, or the night you got the urge to camp out alone in the woods behind the house.

- Put yourself in the position of future generations who will be curious about their ancestor—you—and the life you have led. What would you want them to know about you? What stories would bring your scrapbook to life ten, twenty-five, or even one hundred years from now?

Harness Your Right Brain

Researchers have found that right-brain-dominant people—and probably many scrapbookers—tend to process information through images and feelings, whereas the more logical, left-brain-dominant folks use words. If you are a right-brain thinker, you might find it hard to transfer your thoughts to the page. You might even think you can't write well.

Many successful novelists are right-brain thinkers. Perhaps they make such good writers because they have a heightened ability to visualize the scenes, hear the dialogue, and feel the emotions that make good reading. At some point they learned—probably through practice—to put their right-brain images into words. You, too, have a story to tell; why should being right-brained stop you? (See also chapter 5, "Create Your Memoir as a Graphic Novel," for another right-brain approach to memoir writing.)

The key is to find what works for you. For example, you could start small by writing down what comes to mind, putting it aside, and adding to it later. Or, take a walk while you "picture" your story and how it would flow—then tell the story to your computer later using voice-recognition software, which will type it up for you.

As the ideas begin flowing, don't panic as you realize you face another challenge: deciding which story to write first. Make a list, if that helps. Start with the story that seems easiest, most fun, most important, or most satisfying to write. Don't spend too much time deciding—just start!

SCRAPBOOK PAGE BY *Lindsey Nutt.*

"The Creek." My daughter Lindsey made this page, which unfolds from a triangle, to capture what playing in the backyard as a child meant to her. She could be anything she wanted—including brave—thanks to a creek and drainage tunnel big enough to walk in.

Find the Story, Then Add Visuals

When you think of scrapbooks, you think of photos, ticket stubs, and other two-dimensional keepsakes—that's what many scrapbooks are all about. But a scrapbook revolving around these props portrays only a small part of a life: the part that comes with pictures. One approach is to look at the photos you have and to write down the stories they bring to mind. I challenge you to bend your mind in another direction: **think about the *other* part of your life, the part that no one photographed.**

For example, what experiences would you say were life changing? What are the funny stories that your family tells over and over, or the ones your grandmother told you? You might overlook these stories because you *think* you don't have a way to illustrate them. You have no photos of the stories gathering dust in closets or yellowing in old albums. Use your imagination here. Take cell phone photos of fishing rods, marbles, or other images that you associate with each story. Or find a piece of fishing line or snippet of fabric. Use these items instead of photos to add visual interest to your stories.

The internet is another good source of photos and graphics. You might want to tell the story of the grizzly bear that visited your family's campsite in the Arizona mountains, but no one asked the bear to stick around for a photo. No problem! You can find images of the mountain scenery you remember—and plenty of grizzlies—with a quick internet search.

A word of caution here: You have to assume that photos, drawings, or other images on the internet are protected by copyright. You can make "fair use" of them in a scrapbook for your personal use that you share with family

"The Dress." My sister-in-law Amy's scrapbook features an origami wedding dress that folds up to reveal a story: With the wedding only weeks away, Amy still hadn't found a dress. Her mother Nancy helped search from hundreds of miles away. Finally, Amy found a dress she liked and called her mother. Her mother said she had found a dress, too. As they described the dresses, they realized they had bought the same dress.

and friends. But if you post your pages online or on a site that receives ad revenue, you might violate copyright law. To avoid the risk, look for photos and images in the public domain, such as those on United States government websites. For example, you are likely to find the grizzly bear photo you need on a national park website. The Library of Congress offers a large online collection of photos in the public domain. When you find a photo or image on any website, even a "free" or public domain photo, look for the terms of use that are often at the bottom of the page. Read them carefully and make sure you can comply—or look elsewhere.

The stories that you might not think of telling could be an important part of the family treasure. Your job is to put them into words so they won't be forgotten. Try the strategies in appendix A, "Getting Over Your Fear of Writing," to find the other stories of your life: the turning points, the defining moments, and the fun times, whether or not they exist in photo form. Once you have the stories in mind, you can find ways to illustrate them, as many of the samples in this chapter show. In this age of the internet and cell phone cameras, it's easy to start with the story and add photos and other graphics later.

Your Life in All Its Dimensions

Of course you want to document the good times: the vacations, birthdays, and holidays. They are the stuff scrapbooks are made of. But consider capturing not only the ups, but the downs and in-betweens as well. Together they give a fuller view of your life, with the added gift of your experience and wisdom.

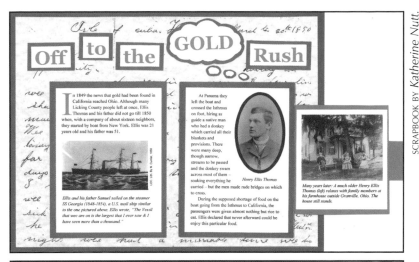

Letters from the Gold Rush. This scrapbook features excerpts from letters that my great-great-grandfather Henry Ellis Thomas wrote during the California Gold Rush. Images from the internet add visual interest. A pull-out tab reveals a photo of the old family home. Introduction by Mary Burnham Thomas, 1907–1999.

  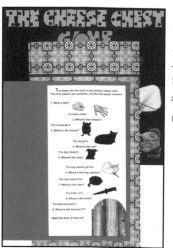

Credit: Katherine Nutt.

The Cheese Chest. My grandmother Eva May Rowley entertained her grandchildren with "The Cheese Chest," a nonsensical question-and-answer game that starts with a tower of hands. I made a scrapbook to show how the game is played.

Some memories are not so pleasant. Your first impulse is to block them out. They might be so personal—or painful—that you'd prefer to keep them to yourself. On the other hand, a memory that shaped you as a person might, from that perspective alone, deserve to be told. As negative as the memory might seem, think about its flip side. You might discover something positive that you didn't realize before, as you bring the perspective of your life experience to the story. Scrapbooking an emotional memory can be truly healing. Here are some examples:

- An event that seemed traumatic at the time—you got lost in the mall food court as a child but kept your wits about you—probably gave you confidence in your ability to take care of yourself.

- Writing about the loss of a relative or pet could lead you to a deeper appreciation of the loved one's special qualities and role in your life and bring peace and reconciliation.

- A disappointment, such as a dead-end job or relationship, might have opened the door to new opportunities and people that you couldn't imagine your life without.

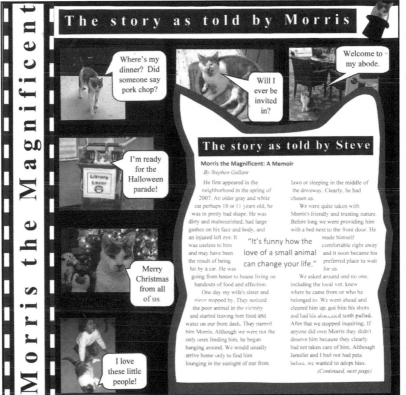

"Morris the Magnificent." My brother Steve wrote a memoir about a cat that he and his wife Jennifer had adopted. Morris was no ordinary cat: he often accompanied my brother, a magician, to his magic shows and served as his assistant and sidekick.

Folds, Flaps, Pull-Outs, and Pockets

By adding stories that narrate your life from many angles and illustrating them in new ways, you have "reinvented" your scrapbook and let your personality shine through.

So how do you organize everything into a pleasing layout? The task poses a particular challenge: finding space. When you set out to combine stories with photos and other graphics, you'll think there isn't room for them all.

That's when you start thinking in 3-D, calling on your right-brain powers to create the fun flaps, folds, pockets, and pull-outs that let you fit more into a smaller space. A number of techniques are illustrated in the scrapbook samples throughout this chapter.

A Scrapbook Primer

Scrapbooking is a passion for many people, as all the books, magazines, websites, and blogs on the topic show. On one hand, the wealth of available materials will instruct and inspire you; on the other, it might overwhelm and block you. You don't have to spend days, or even hours, learning the essentials. A few guidelines will get you started:

Albums

Of the many sizes of scrapbook albums available, you might find that the 12" × 12" size has the most advantages, including more space for your text and photo spreads and a bigger selection of paper. The biggest disadvantage is that you won't be able to print digital layouts from your home computer if the printer can't handle the 12" × 12" sheets; if this is an important consideration, stick with an 8 1/2" by 11" album size. Make sure your album is labeled "archival," which means it is free of the polyvinyl chloride (PVC), lignin, and acid that could damage its contents.

Binding

You have four choices of binding: (a) non-expandable (pages are glued into the album) and (b) expandable strap-bound; (c) post-bound (the posts are large screws); and (d) three-ring. Strap-bound and post-bound albums lay flat when open, allowing you to create two-page spreads without gaps between them. Both allow you to add pages, but they can be difficult to take apart or put back together. To add pages easily, many scrapbookers suggest a three-ring album.

Paper

Card stock, which is stiffer than regular paper, is the background to which you glue photos and other items. Large assortments of scrapbook paper and card stock are available from craft stores or online in individual sheets, pads, or boxes. If you are printing stories, photos, or other elements from your computer, use paper marked with the American National Standards Institute (ANSI) logo, which means it meets ANSI's standards for archival quality.

Writing Tools

Experiment with stamps, stickers, and colored pens for small blocks of words, such as headings and photo captions. Buy them from the scrap-book section of the store so you can be sure they're made with pigment-based ink, which is less likely to fade over time than dye-based ink. Of course, the most efficient way to produce longer passages of text is on a computer. Consumer magazines and websites have compared how well different brands of printer toner and ink cartridges reproduce photos and withstand fading. The results suggest that you should stick with the brand-name inks recommended by your printer's manufacturer. These brands compare well with each other, but often perform better than generic (and less expensive) brands.

Glue/Adhesives

You'll have a daunting number of glue tubes, bottles, spray cans, and "dots" to choose from, so read labels carefully. For example, a "repositionable" or "removable" adhesive allows you to peel up a photo and put it down again multiple times in search of its perfect spot. Use an acid-free photo glue stick to attach stories to backgrounds (use sparingly so the paper doesn't buckle) and try sticky two-sided tabs for attaching photos to mats and backgrounds. If you attach a metal or plastic accessory to your page, you might need a glue other than one that works for gluing paper to paper.

Photos

If you are working with photos in "hard copy," or paper form, the rule of thumb is to copy or scan them and use the copies, not the originals, to cut and crop for your scrapbook. Many printers and scanners now make such high-quality images that it's hard to tell the difference between an original and a copy. If you are taking your own photos rather than using existing ones, a digital camera is your best bet so you can crop and size your photos digitally. Most cell phones double as digital cameras, and some even have zoom and flash capabilities. Read product specifications and customer reviews to help you choose the cell phone with the camera capabilities you want.

Other Supplies

Your supply cabinet should also include a sharp pair of scissors, a paper cutter, and a ruler or straight edge, preferably metal. Add supplies as you need them. You'll be better able to judge the usefulness of those (often expensive) gadgets at the scrapbook store after you've prepared a few pages with what you have.

Design

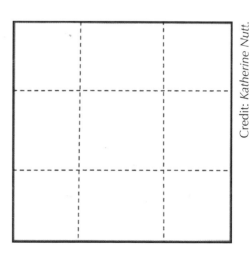

Credit: Katherine Nutt.

To create well-balanced layouts, think of the page as divided vertically and horizontally into thirds by imaginary lines. Decide which photo or other graphic **Focal points.** Imagine lines dividing a scrapbook page into thirds. Place the most important element of your layout—such as a photo, map, or title—near one of the intersections. The eye will be drawn to it.

will be your "focal point" and place it near where two of the lines meet. Group related material or accents together. Repeat visual elements.

Style

Browse almost any book, magazine, or website on scrapbooking and you might think your pages have to be "vintage," "pop," "deco," or "classic," among many other styles; they don't. Find your own style, and don't be discouraged if you have trouble realizing your vision at first. With practice, you'll close the gap between how you imagine the page and your ability to produce it. Embrace the trial and error approach to scrapbooking. Imitate and be inspired by others, but don't worry about whether you could win a prize for artistic talent. With practice, you might!

Working with Aging Albums and Scrapbooks

Many of us have aging albums from our childhoods. The older we are, the more yellowed and brittle the pages have become. The square photos, snapped with our inexperienced hands and first (plastic) cameras, are of shaky quality and arranged in unimaginative, straight rows. They are fixed to the page with corner mounts, if we're lucky, or glue and scotch tape, if we're not. Is it possible to rescue and even transform these crumbling treasures from the past? Yes!

If the album has removable pages—and if you can find page protectors in the right size (check online if your craft store doesn't have them)—put the pages into protectors to guard against further damage. Write your stories and add them to flaps and folds using the ideas and samples in this chapter. Or, make new pages for the stories and insert them between the original pages.

Copy or scan the pages and use all or part of them to make a new scrapbook. If the original pages are too big for your home scanner, visit the nearest self-serve copy center. There you can color-copy the pages onto 11" × 17" paper, which should be white (to keep the original colors intact), or bring your own 12" × 12" scrapbook paper. Adjust the settings to "custom" paper size. You might need to reduce the image slightly to fit everything in. You can also scan images onto a flash drive, so you can work with sections of the page at home.

Try removing the photos and other items from the pages (very carefully!). You might be surprised to find handwritten notes on the backs. To avoid tearing the photos, leave them pasted to the page and cut around them, if necessary. Then glue them back down onto fresh archival quality paper and put them into a new album with page protectors. You could choose to make the new pages look as much like the originals as possible (especially if someone else created them), or to rearrange and update them in a new layout with stories.

Before you start, consider using a digital camera or cell phone to photograph the pages so you'll have a permanent record of what they looked like. When your project is finished, make a note in the scrapbook to tell what you know about the original version (who made it and when). For example, "This scrapbook was created by my mother, Myra Gallant, in the late 1970s with artwork and photos saved from our childhoods."

Credit: Katherine Nutt.

"The Grizzly Bear." Give your old album a makeover by mixing old and new. In this album, I preserved photos from a childhood camping trip but added a favorite family story that was missing about a bear's visit to our campsite. The backing is a magnetic sheet from the craft store, and the figures and cooler have magnets attached to them so they can be moved around.

Scrapping Your Memoirs Digitally

Digital scrapbooking—which simply means using the computer to make a scrapbook or parts of it—can save time and make adding stories to your layouts easier. How much or how little you use the computer depends on your computer skills and preferences.

At the very least, if you have a computer, you'll probably want to use a word processing program to write your stories. Use textboxes to fit your stories into the space you've designed for them. You'll find access to the internet useful for downloading images or photos that would make your pages more visual, as in many of the examples in this chapter.

To dabble a little more in the digital world, you could join a scrapbook community—often for free—that offers software and templates for creating your scrapbooks online. Some online resources, for example, allow you to choose the size of scrapbook you want and pick from available themes and styles to create the pages. Or they allow you to create your book from scratch by importing your own photos and images. You can add text by typing into textboxes or copying and pasting stories from your personal files. Depending on the website's terms of use, which you should always check and abide by, you can share your scrapbook with other members of the community, email it, place an order to have it printed in an album and shipped to you, or print it yourself.

If your computer skills are advanced and you want to fully digitize your scrapbooks, you can purchase scrapbooking software for your computer. This is the trickiest option because you have to buy the version of the software that matches your operating system, which needs to have enough memory and meet other requirements. Prices range from under ten dollars for the simplest programs—which might be worth the low price to see what features you really need—to hundreds of dollars for professional graphics and photo editing software, such as Adobe Photoshop. (The less expensive Adobe Photoshop Elements is geared more for home use.) Popular scrapbooking software includes MyMemories Suite by StoryRock, Inc.; Memory Mixer by Lasting

Impressions for Paper; and CraftArtist Scrapbooks by Serif, all for well under fifty dollars. Check reviews to decide among many options.

Mini-Memoir Scrapbooks as Gifts and Keepsakes

Many scrapbooks end up in dark closets or on the shelf. What if they could hang on a wall, hold jewelry or golf tees, or double as decorative knick-knacks? They can, in the form of posters, calendars, greeting cards, boxes, clipboards, and many other items.

Because you might have even less space for words in one of these forms than in a scrapbook, you don't have to write long stories; a few memorable quotes or moments, or highlights of memoirs yet to be written, might be enough. Use a scrapbook technique to create one of these "mini-memoirs" for yourself or someone who helped make your memories, as in the examples below.

A Memory Greeting Card for a Special Relative or Friend

A greeting card can be a fun way to share your memories with others, especially the people who are part of them. The example here shows a card I made for my "Auntie" Charlotte to remember the good times my brother and I had as children when we visited her in Cleveland, Ohio. The pictures on the card—scanned photos of us and other images from the internet—show some of the fun activities Auntie Charlotte always planned: the zoo, library story hour, an afternoon with a friend who collected penguin figurines, and a Shakespeare play. I also included brief stories of memorable moments.

Credit: Katherine Nutt.

Adventures with Auntie Charlotte. Make a card for a friend or relative to reminisce about your good times together. In this card for my aunt, I included a photo I took with my cell phone of a peanut butter sandwich—Auntie Charlotte always packed peanut butter and butter (not jelly) sandwiches for early morning road trips.

I created the card as an adult, but children would also enjoy depicting stories about themselves and their families in mini-scrapbook form (see chapter 7, "Nurturing the Young Storyteller," for ideas on interviewing grandparents and other relatives).

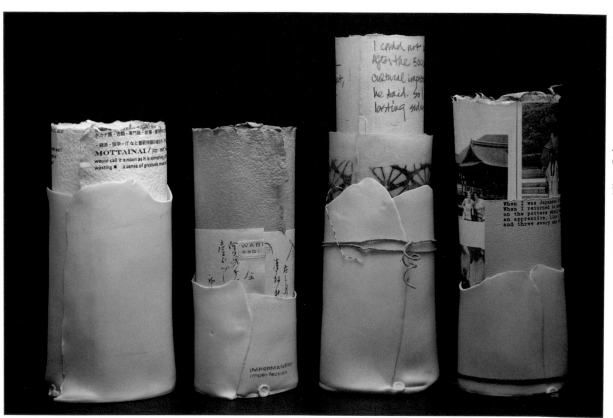

SCULPTURE BY *Nina Gaby.* PHOTO BY *Ben DeFlorio.*

Scraps. Artist Nina Gaby's 3-D memoir vessels are inspiring reminders that memoir can be thought of in new ways. Nina uses paper thin sheets of translucent porcelain to hold her creations, but she suggests a vase, bowl, or even beverage glass as an alternative. In this series, *When I was Japanese,* she documents a vivid period in her life as a young art student, living in Japan, studying ceramics, and learning the hard way about cross-cultural relationships.

Memory Clipboards, Boxes, and Other Items

Browse the wood and paperboard aisles of your craft store for boxes of all shapes and sizes, clipboards, trays, plaques, and many other objects waiting to be scrapbooked. At the end of fifth grade, my daughter Sarah decorated a clipboard as a thank you present for her teacher. She printed images from the internet: a background of colorful marbles to represent the marble jar that Mrs. Smith used as an incentive for good class behavior (when the jar was full, the class held a party); a Nancy Drew book cover, because Sarah read so many of the mysteries that the teacher called her "Nancy"; and a horse, because Sarah and the teacher shared a love of horses. (Printing the images from the internet was "fair use" because the gift was for personal use.) To protect the surface when she was finished, Sarah découpaged the clipboard by brushing it with Mod Podge, a glue-like varnish that seals the surface. Sarah reported that Mrs. Smith was so touched when she opened the gift that her eyes filled with tears!

Almost any item—calendars, mugs, even T-shirts—can be personalized to become a scrapbook-inspired memoir. You can even make a quilted scrapbook (see chapter 6, "Memory Quilts: A Way to Celebrate Lives"). Don't forget to photograph or make copies of your creations for your own scrapbook!

Keep in Mind

- If you're a visual thinker who relates better to pictures than to words, try creating a memoir in the form of a scrapbook to which you add stories of any length.

- The more you write, the more interesting your scrapbook will be to others. You'll benefit, too, by gaining a better understanding of the events, people, and places in your life as you write about them.

- Try different ways to start the stories flowing. Imagine what you would say about a photo or scrapbook page as you show it to a friend or relative. Write about the important moments, people, or places in your life for which you don't have photos.

- Consider capturing not only the good times of your life—the ups—but the downs and in-betweens as well. You might discover that even a negative memory often has a positive side that will reveal itself as you write about it.

- Showcase your stories on folds, flaps, pop-ups, and pull-outs—or hide the more personal ones in secret pockets that you add to your scrapbook page.

- You don't have to know a lot about scrapbooking to get started. Start with a few basics and a trial and error approach. Don't be discouraged if you have trouble making your visions come true. You can always redo what you aren't satisfied with.

- Use the computer, as little or as much as you wish, to make scrapbooking easier: word process your stories; search the internet for photos, maps, and other images; join an online scrapbooking community; or buy scrapbooking software.

- Use a scrapbook and decoupage technique to make "mini-memoirs" in the form of greeting cards, clipboards, calendars, boxes—your imagination is the limit—to give as gifts and keep as practical or fun mementos.

Chapter 5
CREATE YOUR MEMOIR AS A GRAPHIC NOVEL

—— *By Natasha Peterson* ——

Illustrations by Natasha Peterson

Like so many crafts, cartooning is fun. It's satisfying, and it's a remarkably unique form of self-expression. When you illustrate your own memoirs, you go far beyond cartooning, entering the bold and infinitely creative world of graphic stories. No two are alike.

DO YOU LIKE TO DRAW? DO YOU DOODLE THROUGH MEETINGS AND PHONE CALLS?

EVEN WHEN YOU WERE A LITTLE KID, DID YOU LOVE ARTS AND CRAFTS AS MUCH AS RECESS?

DID YOU LOVE THE CHILDREN'S BOOK *HAROLD AND THE PURPLE CRAYON* AND REALLY LOVE HOW HAROLD WOULD ILLUSTRATE HIS OWN STORY AS IT WENT ALONG?

IF THAT'S A YES, THEN YOU MIGHT WANT TO CREATE YOUR MEMOIR AS A GRAPHIC NOVEL.

MEMOIRS AS GRAPHIC NOVELS USED TO BE RARE, BUT THEY ARE QUICKLY BECOMING AS POPULAR AS COMIC BOOKS. TODAY, YOU CAN ND GRAPHIC NOVELS IN SCHOOLS AND PUBLIC LIBRARIES, IN BOOKSTORES AND ONLINE.

GRAPHIC NOVELS, MANY OF THEM MEMOIRS, ARE NALLY BEING ACCLAIMED BY EVEN THE MOST HARD-NOSED CRITICS AS A NEW LITERARY GENRE. SOME GRAPHIC MEMOIRS HAVE BECOME FAMOUS, LIKE *PERSEPOLIS* BY MARJANE SATRAPI, *MARCH* BY JOHN LEWIS, ANDREW AYDIN, AND NATE POWELL, EISNER AWARD-WINNING *SMILE* BY RAINA TELGEMEIER, NATIONAL BOOK AWARD NALIST *STITCHES* BY DAVID SMALL, AND NBA NALIST *CAN'T WE TALK ABOUT SOMETHING MORE PLEASANT?* BY ROZ CHAST.

COMICS AND GRAPHIC NOVELS—WHAT'S THE DIFFERENCE?

THE BIG QUESTION THAT COMES UP OVER AND OVER IS THIS: SO WHAT'S THE DIFFERENCE BETWEEN A GRAPHIC NOVEL AND A COMIC BOOK?

BOTH COMIC BOOKS AND GRAPHIC NOVELS ARE ILLUSTRATED STORIES, AND BOTH FEATURE NARRATION THAT APPEARS AS CAPTIONS, DIALOGUE, AND/OR THOUGHT BUBBLES.

COMIC BOOKS, HOWEVER, ARE ALMOST ALWAYS PART OF A SERIES (VOL.1, NO.3, ETC.), THAT REVOLVES AROUND A SUPERHERO AND VILLAIN. COMIC BOOKS ALSO COMPLY WITH STRICT GUIDELINES FOR THE SIZE OF THE COMIC, LENGTH OF THE STORY, FONTS FOR THE CAPTIONS AND DIALOGUE, AND COMPUTER SOFTWARE FOR INKING IN COLORS. WHEW. THAT'S A LOT OF GUIDELINES TO FOLLOW.

GRAPHIC NOVELS ARE DIFFERENT, BECAUSE THEY DO NOT NEED TO FOLLOW THE GUIDELINES THAT DE NE COMIC BOOKS.

YOU ARE CONSIDERED THE "CREATOR" OF YOUR GRAPHIC NOVEL, WHICH MEANS YOU CAN WRITE ABOUT ANYTHING YOU WANT AND ILLUSTRATE YOUR STORY YOUR WAY.

MY RST GRAPHIC NOVEL, *THE 9-11 STORY BOOK,* AROSE FROM MY HUSBAND'S MEMORY OF WITNESSING THE 2001 ATTACK ON NEW YORK CITY AT GROUND ZERO. SEE . . . HERE HE IS.

AND EVEN THOUGH I WROTE THE STORY, I DIDN'T FEEL LIKE MY DRAWINGS WERE GOOD ENOUGH FOR THE SUBJECT MATTER, SO I WORKED WITH A REAL ARTIST (ACTUALLY, A FRIEND FROM HIGH SCHOOL) WHO MADE THE STORY COME TO LIFE.

ILLUSTRATION BY ALAN GERSON.

ILLUSTRATION BY ALAN GERSON.

I WROTE THE STORY BECAUSE, AFTER THE DISASTER, I HAD SO MUCH EMOTION INSIDE OF ME ABOUT THE ENTIRE EVENT, I HAD TO DO SOMETHING WITH ALL THOSE FEELINGS. I NEEDED TO EXPRESS MYSELF AND GET ALL THAT NEGATIVITY OUT. SO I CREATED A SCARY NARRATOR, AN ANGRY ANGEL OF LIFE AND DEATH, WHO TELLS THE STORY. MY POINT-OF-VIEW ABOUT THE EVENTS OF THAT DAY IS EXPRESSED BY THE NARRATOR, WHO TELLS THE STORY WITH A LOT OF ATTITUDE. HE'S ANGRY AND SARCASTIC, JUST LIKE I WAS.

AFTER IT WAS COMPLETED, I FELT A LOT BETTER AS THOUGH THE EMOTIONS I HAD BEEN CARRYING HAD BEEN TRANSFERRED OUT OF ME AND INTO THE GRAPHIC NOVEL. THAT'S A BEAUTIFUL THING ABOUT DOING YOUR MEMOIR IN GRAPHIC NOVEL STYLE.

ANOTHER TOTALLY BEAUTIFUL THING IS THIS: THERE ARE NO RULES! IT'S ALL ABOUT CREATING YOUR MEMOIR WITH ALL THE CREATIVITY, WIT, AND EMOTION YOU WANT, SO THAT OTHERS WILL NOT ONLY READ IT, BUT SEE IT LIKE YOU DID THROUGH YOUR ILLUSTRATIONS. WHEN YOU COMBINE PERSONAL ILLUSTRATIONS WITH YOUR MEMORIES, THE RESULT CAN BE VERY POWERFUL, AND CAPTIVATING.

CHECK OUT THE DIFFERENCE: "HE DRONED ON, AND EVEN THOUGH IT LOOKED LIKE I WAS LISTENING, I HAD ACTUALLY LEFT MY BODY." OR . . .

YOU CAN EVEN SHOW WHAT YOUR THOUGHTS ARE WITHOUT USING ANY NARRATION BY USING A THOUGHT BUBBLE INSTEAD. FOR EXAMPLE:

DO IT YOUR WAY!

EVERYBODY HAS HIS OR HER OWN WAY OF CREATING A GRAPHIC MEMOIR. SOME FOLKS WRITE THE STORY BEGINNING TO END AND THEN GO BACK AND ILLUSTRATE IT. OTHER PEOPLE DO THE OPPOSITE. THEY START THE ILLUSTRATIONS AND CAPTIONS FROM THE GET-GO, OFTEN DOING A DRAFT RST ON PLAIN PAPER, AND THEN A NAL DRAFT ON CARD STOCK. HERE'S ANOTHER EXAMPLE OF THE SAME PARAGRAPH WRITTEN AND THEN TRANSLATED INTO GRAPHIC NOVEL FORM:

I WAS SEVENTEEN, AND THANKSGIVING DINNER WAS IN SEVENTEEN HOURS. ALONE AT LAST, I WAS WATCHING THE ANNUAL TWILIGHT ZONE MARATHON WHEN MOTHER CAME IN. UNCLE RAD WAS WAITING AT THE AIRPORT, AND I HAD TO GO PICK HIM UP. I CRINGED. THAT OLD POTHEAD SMELLED LIKE A CAT BOX.

MIX IT UP! YOU CAN ADD GRAPHIC NOVEL-STYLE ILLUSTRATIONS AND CARTOONS TO YOUR SCRAPBOOKS AND EVEN AS AN ACCOMPANIMENT TO YOUR FAMILY RECIPES.

CHILDREN ARE NATURAL CARTOONISTS, OFTEN SO EAGER TO DRAW WHAT'S AROUND THEM AND ADD THEIR EXPLANATION (OR CAPTION). WHAT FUN TO I NCLUDE CHILDREN'S ILLUSTRATED AND CAPTIONED ADDITIONS TO FAMILY MEMOIR PROJECTS!

GRAPHIC MEMOIR ELEMENTS

THERE ARE SEVERAL PARTS TO A GRAPHIC MEMOIR/NOVEL:

1. NARRATION. THAT'S YOU TELLING YOUR STORY AS YOU REMEMBER IT. YOU ARE THE NARRATOR, AND THE STORY IS FROM YOUR POINT OF VIEW. IN MEMOIR, THE NARRATION IS MOST OFTEN WRITTEN IN THE RST PERSON. NARRATION CAN BE WITHIN THE BORDERS OF THE ILLUSTRATION, OR NEXT TO IT LIKE A CAPTION.

2. ILLUSTRATIONS. LARGE, SMALL, IN THE MARGINS, LLING THE WHOLE PAGE, BLACK/WHITE OR IN COLOR, BEAUTIFUL, JARRING, SIMPLE, DETAILED. THE SKY'S THE LIMIT.

3. DIALOGUE. DIALOGUE IS DRAWN WITHIN THE CELL WHEN ONE OR MORE CHARACTERS ARE TALKING, CONTAINED IN A DIALOGUE BUBBLE.

4. THOUGHT BUBBLES. MANY ILLUSTRATORS USE DOTTED LINES FOR THOUGHT BUBBLES TO SEPARATE THEM FROM DIALOGUE. AND SOMETIMES, THERE'S A FTH ELEMENT . . .

5. ANNOTATED NOTES ALONG THE SIDE WITH ADDITIONAL INFORMATION.

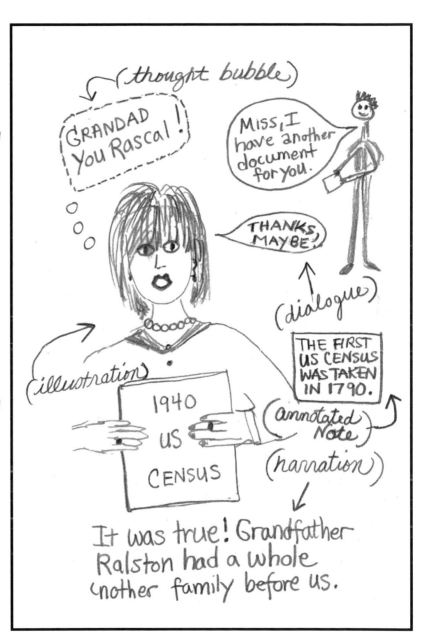

GETTING STARTED: TOOLS YOU'LL NEED

If you are thinking, "I need something to draw on and something to draw with," you're not far off. Still, it's a little more complicated than that.

PENS OR PENCILS

You have to gure out if you're more comfortable working with a pencil or pen. Really, you have to play around with soft No. 2 pencils, art pencils, and even mechanical pencils, and see which one feels best to you. You might want to use different pencils (or pens) for drawing and lettering. While you're testing out pencils, test out erasers, too, because you'll need them.

The same goes for pens. Classic white-out will get you through your errors.

PAPER

When it comes to your sketchbook, the most commonly used paper for graphic novels is Bristol "board." Bristol is somewhere in thickness between copier paper and cardboard, and it comes in a smooth nish and a rougher "vellum" nish. It doesn't stop there, however. You'll also have to decide on your sketchbook size, and whether you'll create one cell per page or have several.

SOFTWARE

You can also create your graphic novel on a computer. You can color your illustrations in two ways: do it yourself with ink or paint and scan each one into your computer, or scan in your drawings and add color to them with "inking" software.

You can even create your own font from your own handwritten letters and numbers once they are scanned into your computer. New, inexpensive software enables you to create and work with your own font on a Mac or PC. This makes rewriting a lot more manageable, because you can key in your edits.

Once your memoir is completed, scan all your pages into your computer. Another step some people take is to work with a graphic designer, who can add page numbers and pull all your elements together digitally. I did this with my graphic novel, because I wanted a version that I could post online, in addition to a printed version.

Then, you can have your book bound and printed—as many copies as you would like! You can use a local of ce supply store to do this (most of them have printing services), or search for printing companies online. A company that specializes in illustrated books, including comic books, is a good choice.

THERE ARE ALSO NUMEROUS DIGITAL-ONLY COMIC BOOK AND GRAPHIC NOVEL WEBSITES. IF YOU WANT, YOU CAN UPLOAD YOUR GRAPHIC MEMOIR TO ONE OR MORE OF THESE SITES, SO FOLKS CAN READ IT ONLINE. PLUS, YOU'LL ALWAYS HAVE A READY LINK TO YOUR WORK.

FOR INSPIRATION, STUDY A FEW POPULAR GRAPHIC NOVELS. AS YOU READ, TAKE NOTE OF ALL THE DIFFERENT WAYS THE MAIN ELEMENTS (NARRATION, DIALOGUE, ETC.) ARE HANDLED.

ULTIMATELY, PENCIL IN HAND, IT'S YOUR STORY. IMAGINATION UNLIMITED!

KEEP IN MIND

- LIKE CREATING ANY MEMOIR, CREATING YOURS AS A GRAPHIC NOVEL CAN BE EMOTIONAL AND SATISFYING.

- GRAPHIC NOVELS DON'T HAVE THE SAME GUIDELINES AS COMIC BOOKS. THERE AREN'T ANY FORMAL RULES; IT'S WHATEVER WORKS WELL FOR YOU.

- YOU CAN WRITE UP YOUR MEMOIR AND THEN ILLUSTRATE IT, OR DO YOUR ILLUSTRATIONS RST AND CAPTION THEM WITH YOUR STORY.

- TEST OUT PENCILS, PENS, PAPER, AND ERASERS—OR COMPUTER SOFTWARE—TO ND OUT WHAT FEELS BEST TO YOU.

- MEMOIRS AS GRAPHIC NOVELS ARE MORE POPULAR THAN EVER.

- HAVE A BALL CREATING YOUR MEMOIR!

Chapter 6
MEMORY QUILTS: A WAY TO CELEBRATE LIVES

— By Linda Pool —

In this chapter, you will learn how to share family stories in a tangible way by transforming your memories into quilts that can be passed down generation after generation.

The much-loved tradition of using up instead of throwing out has been adopted in the craft-turned-art of quilting. This chapter helps you choose a theme and create your own memoir quilt from keepsakes and clothes.

Plus, it gives practical advice on how to use images to incorporate bits of vintage documents and photos into your quilts. Friends and family benefit from these unique ways of storytelling.

Choosing Your Quilt Theme

If you sew or craft, quilting offers you a way to turn your art into memoir. Quilting is one of the most diverse and practical ways to capture the stories of your life or the life of a loved one. A quilt will be cherished for generations. Even after it's no longer used for warmth and comfort, it might be hung on a rack or on a wall and the beauty and charm of its design will live on.

Of all the inspirations for memoir quilts, the challenge is to choose just one subject or idea, one person, or one family as the theme and focal point of your quilt. Ideas can come from many different places: a special memory, a family holiday, a friend's wedding, or the loss of a loved one or a special pet. Regardless of where the ideas come from, memoir quilts can serve important purposes: healing, preserving family history, and memorializing loved ones. The possibilities are endless and someone is always excited to receive a quilt full of memories.

Memories Are a Good Starting Place

Memorable moments are good starting places for creating a quilt that tells a story. Happy memories and the joy of life shared with others lead us to want to create something tangible, something that we can put our hands on as a reminder of the special moments we have shared with family and friends.

Sad memories, too, can be used in a memoir quilt to bring closure and comfort after an unexpected or traumatic event.

What kinds of moments might inspire a story quilt?

Celebrations are memorialized in scrapbooks all the time. How about making a quilt to tell the story of your family's holiday celebrations or other special events, like vacations? You could include opera ticket stubs from Vienna, Austria; football tickets from the Orange Bowl; Mickey Mouse's autograph; and other scraps that remind you of happy times spent with those you love. Combine these images with a few words describing the most memorable parts of these events, print them onto fabric, and sew them into your quilt.

A wedding quilt, a centuries-old tradition, could be the basis for a memoir quilt that tells the story of the happy couple's first meeting, significant milestones, the best man's toast at the wedding, and other meaningful moments in their lives.

Pets are another favorite quilt theme. Fun stories and pictures of the animals you have loved, or of one special pet, when transferred to fabric, could be stitched into a lovely little quilt.

Hobbies are another starting place for remembered moments that tell a story. Imagine the joy you would bring to a boy who loves to play baseball if you made him a quilt that featured a photo of him wearing his uniform and holding his bat, standing tall and proud. Now imagine including a similar photo from each year that he played ball, showing his growth and his changing teams as he has matured. Add a few quotes or highlights of his biggest baseball moments. What a treasure for him!

A wedding memory, 19″ × 20″. These images, photographed at a nephew's outdoor wedding, give charming personal glimpses into the bride's and groom's personalities. Put into a quilt, these memories will bring to mind their very special day whenever they see the quilt hanging on their wall. Quilt by Linda Pool.

PHOTO BY *Willow Bodman.*

Chris's college quilt, 72" × 90". Pictures recalling my son Chris's infancy, school days, hobbies, and even girlfriend at the time are included in this quilt. I made it for my son Chris to use on his college bed. The girlfriend later became his wife. Quilt by Linda Pool.

PHOTO BY *Willow Bodman.*

Chris's baseball moment. This close-up of Chris's college quilt captures one of his team memories from baseball.

Chris's college quilt was made out of my son Chris's cotton shirts that he had worn in his high school years. The photos in the center squares of the quilt included his baby picture; school, sports, and prom photos; and even his girlfriend, who is now his wife.

Travel and places lived make wonderful themes for a memoir quilt. My mother and father, for example, recently traveled to Pennsylvania to visit the places they lived after they married. They photographed each house they had lived in, places where I had lived since my birth. This is a great inspiration for a quilt. And people who are in the military or other occupations that require them to move around might have lived in so many places that, in their mind, they all run together and get mixed up. What happened here, or was it there? It might give a child some form of stability to see an image of each house or apartment that he or she lived in through the years. Each photo might jog a story of a person or event that happened while the family lived in that location.

Careers or hobbies are another rich source of inspiration for a memoir quilt. If you are an artist, for example, you could make a memoir quilt that tells the story of your artwork, using the actual images to create the design. Your growth as an artist might be visible from the changes in your images and subject matter.

I love to take pictures. As a sample for a class that I teach, I made a quilt of my floral photographs. These photographs were taken in tropical, desert, hothouse, home, and many other locations throughout my travels. A label can be included on the back of the quilt to identify the flower and where the picture was taken. This would tell future generations some special things about me. I love flowers and travel!

Quilts That Heal a Loss

Making a quilt can help you heal from traumatic events such as divorce or loss of a loved one.

Divorce. When I think of healing quilts, one of the first quilts that come to mind is a quilt made in May 1991, by Katharine Brainard, just after she found

My travels in florals, 63″ × 63″. Flowers draw my attention wherever I am, so I document my travels with the local vegetation. These photos were taken all over the world. Quilt by Linda Pool.

her husband with his twenty-three-year-old secretary, on his new boat, in a compromising position. She made the quilt to work through her anger, hurt, and disappointment in her unfaithful husband.

Katharine added words and phrases to the quilt by printing and writing them onto the fabric. For example, she used the words "road kill" and made tire track marks on the quilt by actually driving over the quilt fabric with the wheels of her car. This acted-out visual was dramatic enough to help work out some of her destructive feelings.

The quilt has been displayed for the public to see and has elicited different reactions. A husband and wife (therapists and contemporary art collectors) purchased the quilt because they liked its visual appeal, its humor, and "its value as a constructive expression of powerful feelings," as Susan Baer of *The Baltimore Sun* said.

Katharine said she had an enormous sense of relief after she put the last stitch in the quilt. She said she had shared all her feelings about her husband and their divorce through the images on the quilt, and this gave her "closure."

Loss of a child/sibling/parent/friend. The death of someone you love is always a very emotional time in your life. Making a quilt can help you work through the deep feelings you have about the loss of your loved one. Planning and making a quilt gives you time to think about the person you are missing and what he or she meant to you, and it gives your hands something to do while you are thinking. The quilt will be something tangible to hold and snuggle with, bringing you a little closer to that person.

When my brother Daniel passed away in a mountain-climbing accident in Colorado, I took his shirts back to Virginia and made a quilt for his son's tenth

PHOTO BY *Willow Bodman.*

Eric's quilt, 56″ × 87″. This quilt features my brother Daniel's shirt pockets. After Daniel died in a mountain climbing accident, I made the quilt for his son Eric to bring his father "to life." Quilt by Linda Pool.

birthday. Working with the fabrics, I could still smell my brother's fragrance, and this made him a little more alive to me. Making a quilt from the deceased person's clothing will not make the loss any less painful. However, making it for another person is such a positive act that it will help heal your heart.

When Eric recognized the fabrics in the quilt, i.e., his dad's shirts worn so often around the house, the quilt became a precious, up-close reminder that his dad was so much a part of his life. The remembrance this invokes will keep memories alive in a more real way.

Imagine making a quilt with just the pockets of a pile of shirts. What treasures could be put into those pockets? For his son's quilt, the only part I used of my brother Daniel's shirts was the pockets. I later made quilts for my sister-in-law and two nieces with the leftover parts of the shirts.

My brother Daniel rode his bicycle from coast to coast of the United States in 1980, and he wrote a journal entry every day about his experiences along the way. He also wrote journal entries of each of his mountain climbs. His journals were, and still are, a treasure for the family he left behind.

Daniel wrote his thoughts on God and life and relationships and the wonder of his experiences with nature. Some of Daniel's comments were perfect for lessons to help his children grow to be happy and emotionally healthy adults. I took some of his words, in his own hand-writing, and also typed them and transferred them onto fabric. I collected photos of Daniel and the family, specifically ones that showed Daniel with his arm around his son or his son sitting on his shoulders, and transferred them onto fabric. I stitched the pieces of fabric to ribbons and placed them in the pockets with the ribbon attached to the pocket edge. This way the words will never get lost and separated from the quilt.

PHOTO BY *Willow Bodman.*

Pocket contents. Excerpts from Daniel's outdoor adventure journal are stuffed into each pocket of the quilt to help Eric know who his father was. On one side of each fabric block is Daniel's handwritten journal entry and on the other side is its typed version. I put pictures of Eric with his father in the pockets with buttons.

My sister-in-law told me one day that the whole family goes to the quilt to reach into the pockets and read Daniel's words or see his picture, and that has helped them to heal from the hurt of his loss.

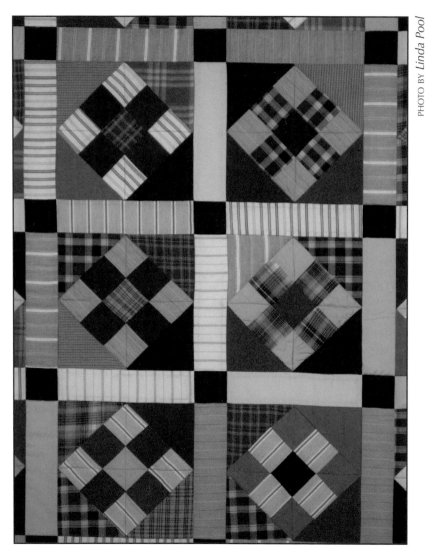

PHOTO BY *Linda Pool*

Christie's quilt, 62″ × 90″. I made two similar quilts for Daniel's daughters with the leftover fabric from the shirts.

Quilts That Preserve Family History

You can also make quilts to preserve family history using photos, documents, correspondence, and other trinkets that trigger memories and, taken together, tell a large (or small) story. First, think of your theme, such as ancestors, and then select the artifacts that will make the quilt a wonderful heirloom. Your artifacts could include photographs, documents (such as a marriage license), correspondence, and/or trinkets or other physical objects that jog memory.

Old sepia-toned photos that have been passed down in the family for generations or just found in grandma's attic can be shared and documented by making a family history quilt. It is a treasure to have a photo history of what your ancestors looked like to conjecture about where Grandma got her big nose, to notice how the men in the family tend to be tall like Great-Grandpa Henry, and to confirm once and for all who actually wore that old dress spotted in a trunk in the attic. Could that really be Aunt Alice wearing it in the photo where she is leaning on the fence watching someone feeding the chickens? What a treasure!

Documents and other important papers could be included in a family history quilt and will add so much more interest and information to the pictures you have used. Do you have a copy of an old marriage license or birth certificate from your ancestors? Maybe you have one of their old school report cards, or a baptism certificate. If you include the names of the people pictured in your quilt, the documents with the names on them will be self-explanatory.

PHOTO BY *Willow Bodman*.

Grandma's report card, 20″ × 26″. This is my maternal grandmother's picture, taken when she would have been in the fourth grade. We found a treasure when we found her fourth-grade school report card. C. 1912/1913. Quilt by Linda Pool.

Correspondence, such as old love letters between your grandparents or a note of commendation sent to your grandfather when he was in the service, copied and included on the quilt, will be a treasured addition. And ***trinkets or other items that jog memory*** can help tell important family stories. My mother-in-law, for example, saved the "Do Not Disturb" sign sporting the logo of the Ritz, the hotel where she and my father-in-law stayed the first night of their honeymoon. The image of the sign is included in a quilt about her and my father-in-law, as it meant a lot to her and she mentioned it to me many times.

PHOTO BY *Willow Bodman.*

The Evans/Pool quilt, 27″ × 26″. Copies of special keepsakes were combined with copies of photos to tell a more complete story of my in-laws. Quilt by Linda Pool.

Adding key words and phrases will create yet another, deeper dimension. If you are making a quilt about a person, you could include words to represent personality traits, such as honest, trustworthy, loving, kind, or giving. If your quilt is about a treasured memory, some of the words you could use might be "baked us cookies," "pushed us on the swing," "gave hugs and kisses," "doctored skinned knees," etc. Your mother or grandmother might have had a favorite saying that she repeated often and that would benefit future generations, such as: "If your dreams turn to dust, vacuum," or "If you want to make friends, be a friend."

PHOTO BY *Willow Bodman.*

Man's suit and tie quilt, 13″ × 19″. My best friend Barb made this little wall-hanging quilt and three others for family members after her father passed away. She made the quilt using her father's best suit and some of his ties. Quilt by Barb Celio.

Friendship Quilts

Signature quilts or autograph quilts are another form of memoir quilt. They are also referred to as "friendship" quilts.

To make a friendship quilt, collect signatures of friends and family on fabric and stitch them into special themed quilts. Record your family names for posterity or make an autograph quilt as encouragement for a friend going through a rough time. Memorialize an event, group, or organization of people by collecting their signatures and stitching them into a signature quilt.

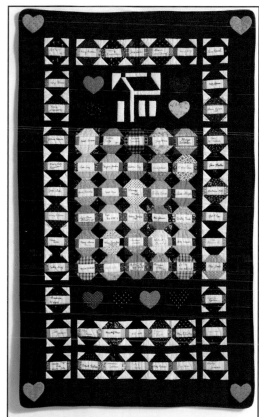

PHOTO BY *Willow Bodman.*

Friendship quilt, 28″ × 46″. Seventy-one of my quilting friends pieced and signed these mini-quilt blocks. Barb Celio stitched them together and gave them to me after my year as president of our local quilt guild. What a joy to look at the names and remember friends who were a part of my life in the guild. Quilt by Linda Pool.

PHOTO BY *Willow Bodman.*

Antique signature block, 12″ × 12″. Signatures can be collected and stitched into quilts for a memoir of groups of people. The signatures were embroidered onto this antique quilt block. For a faster way to get the same effect, prepare your fabric by stabilizing the back with freezer paper, grab a permanent ink pen, and collect the signatures.

Many quilts from the past boast a large sampling of family surnames as groups of people signed fabric and included these signatures into quilt blocks. These signatures not only represented the makers of the quilt blocks, but the participants in an organization, the members of a family, or even in some cases, the signatures of very important people such as the presidents of the United States, political leaders, actors, pastors, and many other groups and clubs. Historians and genealogists study these signature quilts to discern the history and community of certain regions of the country. These signature quilts tell many stories just by knowing who was involved in the creation of the quilt.

Quilts That Memorialize Loved Ones

Creating a quilt that memorializes loved ones not only helps you come to terms with their loss but also creates an heirloom every bit as important as the historical statues or modern websites commonly used for this purpose. And, it's something to carry with you and keep you warm.

When my mother passed away, I collected a lot of her clothes that I thought would work for making quilts and made seven of them, one each for my father, my siblings, myself, Mom's best friend, and a lady that my mother helped raise. The seven quilts all used the same design for the layout. I chose to work with squares. The square is simply one of the easiest and fastest shapes to piece together.

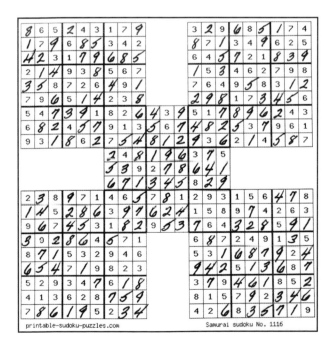

Sudoku drawing. A drawing like this was used for the layout of nine different fabrics for Mom's Clothing Quilts on pages 116 and 117.

But now, what kind of interesting pattern could I use to lay out the fabrics so that the quilt would not just be random squares sewn together? Aha! I remembered the Sudoku puzzle that my daughter, Genelle, had finished when she was home for a visit. It had five blocks of 9 × 9 squares, wherein the five puzzles overlap into one larger puzzle. Numbers are placed in the squares so that no number is repeated in a square of nine or in the lines going vertically or horizontally. Genelle had completed the puzzle successfully, and I asked her for a copy of it. I decided that I would use her completed puzzle as the layout for nine different fabrics in each of the quilts I was making. My parents and siblings loved to play games, so using a game for the quilt's fabric layout was appropriate.

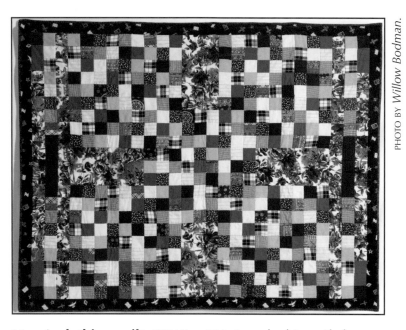

PHOTO BY *Willow Bodman.*

Mom's clothing quilt, 53½″ × 68″. I made this quilt for my father from my mother's "everyday" clothing. Three extra rows of squares at the left and right of the Sudoku layout lengthen the quilt. Quilt by Linda Pool.

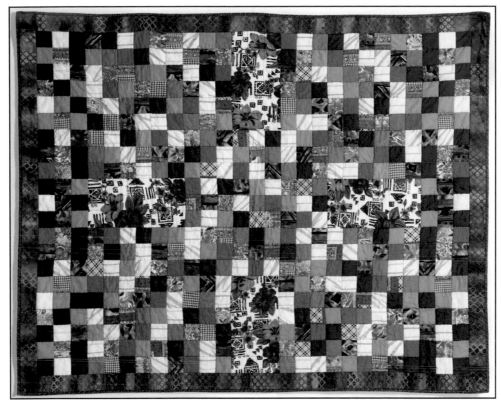

Mom's clothing quilt, 53½" × 68". This quilt uses the same layout of squares as my father's quilt but with different coloration. Quilt by Linda Pool.

This may sound like all the quilts looked alike; however, they were all made using different pieces of clothing, thus different colors and prints, so they were all unique. Some had an overall pink look and some blue. It was fun to lay out the pieces. I chose a number for each of the nine fabrics. As I held the finished Sudoku puzzle in one hand, I laid down the precut fabric squares in the same configuration as the numbers on the puzzle. Since I did not want the quilts to be square, I added three extra rows of blocks and strips of fabric to both ends to make the quilts rectangular.

Now the quilts not only have a very mixed-up layout of colors and prints, they also include a "hidden" puzzle for someone to study and decipher. What fun! A sort of game to keep you occupied while covered with the quilt. All this was created from patches of clothes that I recognized as having been worn by my mother. Seeing the fabrics brings back memories of things we did together while she wore that clothing. I spent about a month working on these seven quilts, and it helped so much to heal from the loss of her.

Choosing Your Fabrics

The best fabrics for a quilt are 100 percent cotton; however, cotton/polyester blends will work. Light-weight fabrics are best. If you want to make a quilt after someone passes away, and would like the quilt to be made from the person's clothing, collect a pile of his or her clothes (both everyday and nice items) that are cotton or cotton blends and are not too thick in weave or texture. You will need solids as well as prints—and lots of color. If using men's shirts, you will need about eight to ten shirts to make a twin-bed-sized quilt.

Jeans

Many quilts have been made from old blue jeans that have worn out or been discarded. Whenever you see a quilt made from jeans, you will see parts with pockets and parts with the golden decorative stitching used on the jeans. These quilts can be rather heavy but are warm and well loved, especially by teenagers. This type of quilt makes a great family room quilt to snuggle under while watching TV.

T-Shirts

What family does not have a pile of T-shirts saved because they have a logo from a beloved sports team, an organization they support, summer camp, a yearly reunion, swim team, a school, etc.? One way to keep and preserve this logo after the shirt is no longer worn is to make a quilt with it.

PHOTO BY *Willow Bodman.*

Don's T-shirt quilt, 56½″ × 66″. Some of my husband's favorite hobbies and interests are memorialized in this T-shirt quilt. It was good to exchange a bag of old T-shirts for a quilt to keep us warm on a cold winter evening in front of the TV. Quilt by Linda Pool.

T-shirt fabric is knit and therefore stretchy. These stretchy fabrics need to be stabilized if used to make a quilt. Purchase an iron-on tricot stabilizer from the local fabric store and iron it to the back of the logo the size of the square or rectangle that you will be cutting from the shirt. It is best to iron on this stabilizer before cutting out the logo. If you purchase the stabilizer intended for knits, the fabric will still feel soft and pliable after it is applied, but will not stretch out of shape. Using this stabilizer will make all the difference in determining whether or not you like the finished quilt.

T-shirt quilts that have not been stabilized will have wrinkles, lumps, and bumps. Take the time to do this important step of stabilizing so that your T-shirt quilt can last a long time and tell the story of the person it was made for.

Conversation Prints

Many fabrics are printed with thematic prints and are called conversation prints. You can find fabrics with sports balls, sports players, makeup items, animals, hobbies, space objects, airplanes, tractors, furniture, baskets, travel, games, food, collectibles, money, old advertisements, cleaning products, movie stars, and just about anything and everything there is that has been printed on fabric. If you find a fabric store with a good supply of these conversation prints, you can include these picture fabrics to explain the hobbies, favorites, and personality of the person you are making the quilt for and about.

Conversation prints are especially interesting for children. They will find an endless supply of interesting things to look at when wrapped up in their quilt.

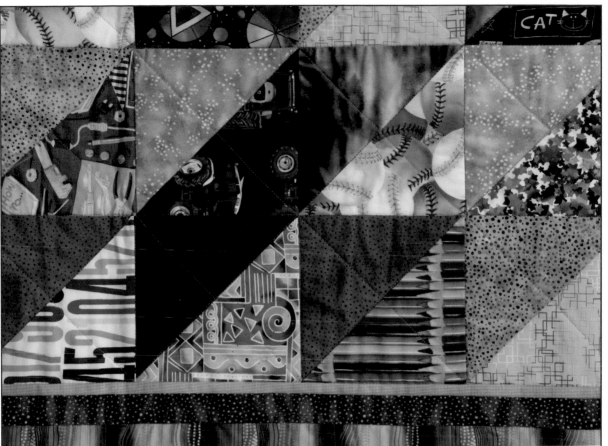

PHOTO BY *Willow Bodman.*

Conversation prints. Children love quilts using fabrics with images of some of their favorite things.

Grandma's Scrap Bag

If your great-grandmother was a quilter, she most likely made her quilts from the family's worn-out clothing or she saved the scraps from making new clothes. If you have inherited her scrap bag, you have a treasure trove of

PHOTO BY *Linda Pool.*

Vintage baskets quilt. My friend had fabrics from the 1920s through 1950s that her mother-in-law had collected. I used them to hand-piece and appliqué 210 different mini basket blocks and made this twin-sized quilt and two wall hangings that I presented to the collector's granddaughters. Gayle Ropp hand-quilted the quilt with the author's designs. Quilt by Linda Pool.

fabrics to use to make a memoir quilt. You may not know who wore which fabric; however, just having a collection of older fabrics is a good starting point for a lovely vintage quilt.

PHOTO BY *Willow Bodman.*

Vintage hearts quilt, 17″ × 21″. These hearts were hand-appliquéd using the same collection of 1920s to 1950s fabrics, as shown in the vintage baskets quilt. Quilt by Linda Pool.

Incorporating Your Stories into the Quilt

Fabrics aren't the only vintage items you can use in creating a memoir quilt. Well-chosen artifacts such as photos, letters, and important papers help you tell your stories and help you make a connection to the past. When I found an old marriage license that belonged to my great grandparents, it was a windfall!

PHOTO BY *Willow Bodman.*

Paternal great-grandparents' marriage license and photo, 1901. I shrank the image of my great-grandparents' marriage license and printed it onto a Printed Treasures fabric sheet along with their photo. The technique is explained in the section "Printing Words and Pictures Directly onto Fabric." I will cut the marriage license and picture apart to use in a quilt.

They actually touched the paper, cherished it, and kept it in a safe place. It is as though I touched their lives in a small way. This special document can still be kept in a safe place even as I use it to tell their story in a memoir quilt.

A Memoir Fabric "Scrap" Book

Try a new concept by making a scrapbook from fabric. Saving scraps and pieces of our family's past is something that most mothers do. We save that cute little baby bonnet, the tiny pair of soft shoes, the bib with the baby's name embroidered on it. You may have a snippet of hair from the baby's

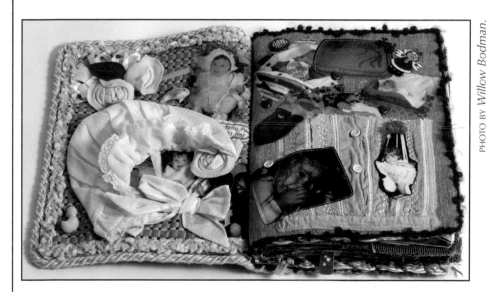

PHOTO BY *Willow Bodman.*

Genelle's fabric scrap book 1, 22″ × 13″. I made this fabric scrapbook for my daughter Genelle and gave it to her at her bridal shower. I included many items from her past, such as her first baby bonnet and a picture of her wearing the bonnet and matching dress. The roses on the page are made from baby socks. The following page has a picture of newborn Genelle under the front panel of one of my maternity dresses. Fabric scrap book by Linda Pool.

first haircut you can put in a little pouch and include on a fabric scrapbook page. Your child may also have a box of saved trinkets. You can sew these treasures, photos copied on fabric, baubles, and all kinds of memorabilia onto the pages of a fabric book for an organized way of displaying these precious memories.

Use decorator fabric samples for the book's pages, with clothing, lace, and doilies as the backdrop for displaying your treasures. Trim pages with

PHOTO BY *Willow Bodman*.

Genelle's fabric scrap book 2, 22″ × 13″. On the left page I strung images of Genelle's baby dresses, stabilized with iron-on Pellon, and tucked them into the pocket of her embroidered bib. The opposite page represents moments she shared with her brother, Kevin. Under the eyelet bib from one of her dresses are three pictures of Kevin wearing Genelle's dresses; she used her little brother as a living doll to dress up while playing. Fabric scrapbook by Linda Pool.

handmade braids, gimp, twill, or ribbon, but don't be too neat. Raw edges are the charm of a fabric scrapbook. Choose a theme for each page, such as father, mother, sister, brother, sports, hobbies, etc. Make mini fabric photo albums to display multiple pictures on a page. Use your imagination and display items in a creative way, such as baby dresses hanging on a clothes line and tucked into a makeshift pocket.

PHOTO BY *Willow Bodman*.

Stephanie's fabric scrap book, 22″ × 13″. This book belongs to my daughter, Stephanie. On the left page are her baby dress and pictures of her wearing it while held by her brother, Chris. On the right are her bonnet and a doll's drawers used as the pocket for holding little cloth bags of snippets of her "spun-gold" baby hair. Fabric scrap book by Linda Pool.

Photo Quilt Layouts

Photos are wonderful additions to a memoir quilt. Let's look at how you can use photos, fabric, and fabric panels to create interesting patterns.

Simple Photo Layouts

When you make a quilt using photos, the design for the quilt should be kept simple. The photos will be the main interest of the quilt, and you would not want to detract from the viewer's appreciation of them by having an intricately pieced block. Words can be typed to fit the size of the spaces in your quilt block squares and then transferred onto fabric to stitch on the front or back of the quilt. These words will help to tell the story of your photos in the quilt.

Search for quilt block designs that have open squares in the middle of the block. This is a good location for a photo or words. Other quilt block designs have squares at each corner. This layout might work as well. These three blocks are all drawn using a nine-patch design. Each whole block is divided into 3 × 3 squares and then divided further for working with its distinct block design.

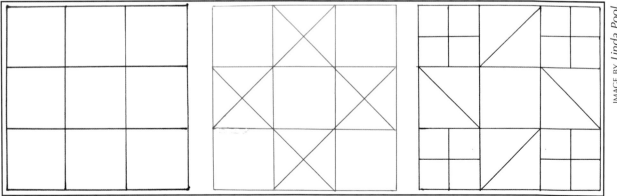

IMAGE BY *Linda Pool.*

Simple quilt blocks. The center square and corner squares of these quilt blocks are good spots to place the pictures for a memoir quilt.

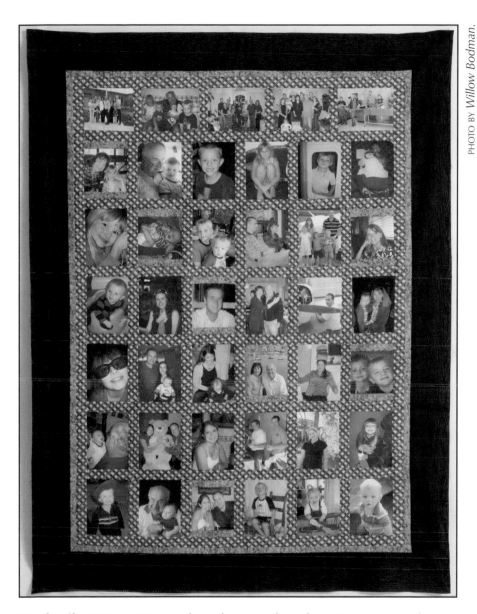

PHOTO BY *Willow Bodman.*

My family, 35″ × 47″. I gathered some of my favorite pictures of my children and grandchildren, inkjet-printed them onto treated fabric for permanency, and included them in this colorful quilt. Quilt by Linda Pool.

Adding Fabrics

Be sure the fabrics you add to surround the photo block don't detract from the photo. Use colors that complement the colors in the photo and keep the fabric prints simple or low-contrast so as not to draw the eye away from the photos.

PHOTO BY *Willow Bodman.*

Chris's house quilt. When making a house design quilt, stitch fabric pictures into windows and doors to give the impression that people live there. Here are pictures of my son Chris and of me holding him in my arms. Quilt by Linda Pool.

In a house quilt made for my son Chris, I added photo transfers in the windows and doors of the houses. The photos are an afterthought as they do not stand out with the bright colors of the houses and roofs. In this case, this is as it should be; the people look like they are inside the houses. That's me holding Chris in the window.

PHOTO BY *Willow Bodman.*

Family tree, 26½″ × 36″. It was fun to play with this tree-design fabric panel, to which I added ironed-on photos to make it a true "family tree." Quilt by Linda Pool.

Photo Montage

You might even want to make a photo memory quilt that is not in the form of blocks but that has an overall layout of pictures. You may like the idea of appliquéing a tree to a light colored fabric and using the iron-on heat transfer technique to apply the photos directly to the background fabric as leaves on the tree.

PHOTO BY *Willow Bodman.*

School days. I purchased these fabric panels to make a fabric book with ironed-on images. I changed my mind about making a book and will include these framed photos in a quilt instead.

Printed Fabric Panels

Sometimes you can find fabrics printed with panels of bordered empty spaces meant to be used as signature blocks for labeling your quilts. There might be a dozen or more different designs on a panel. You can transfer your photos directly into these bordered spaces.

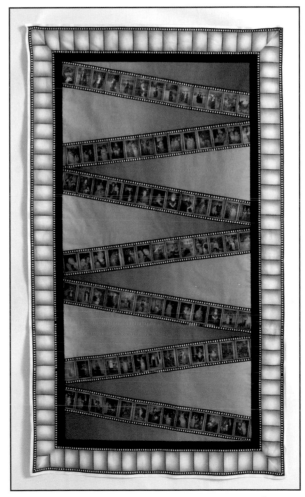

PHOTO BY *Willow Bodman.*

Film strip quilt, 22″ × 38″. I picked out multiple images of my daughter Stephanie and me in period costumes, printed them out using my computer's CAMEDIA Master program (index size), and printed them onto heat transfer paper. Then I cut each to fit one of the filmstrip-frame spaces and ironed them onto the fabric. Quilt by Linda Pool.

When I found this fabric, which resembles the film used to make movies, I used the blank spaces for transferred images. The "filmstrip" contains photos of my daughter Stephanie, me, and some of our friends in period attire for historic reenactments.

PHOTO BY *Willow Bodman.*

Family heritage quilt, 50″ × 64″. These ironed-on images were fit into the frames of this pre-printed fabric intended for making a fabric book. Repurposing the fabric panels made this a wonderful quilt. Pearls were hand-stitched to the frames. Quilt by Linda Pool.

This panel was intended to be stitched into a fabric book with photos ironed onto the fabric pages, but I made it into a whole quilt instead. Notice how the photos do not fit exactly into the white bordered space. This does not mar the look of the overall quilt block. You can also group smaller photos inside one frame.

Now, let's talk about transferring photos.

PHOTO BY *Willow Bodman.*

Family heritage quilt close-up. This block combines my husband Don's picture as a two- to three-year-old and my picture as a five-year-old. You can group smaller photos inside one frame to take advantage of the space and incorporate as many images as you can to tell the story. Quilt by Linda Pool.

PHOTO BY *Willow Bodman.*

Floral-bordered photo. I ironed this image of a charming little girl onto an empty floral frame, one of the many different floral frames printed on this fabric panel.

Preparing Images for Transfer

The first thing I need to say here is that you are NOT going to ruin any of your old or new photos or documents by doing any of the processes that I am about to discuss. You will only be using the photos and documents to make copies. They will either be scanned into the computer or laid onto the surface of a flat-bed printer for copying. Breathe freely! You will NOT lose your originals.

You will need a program for your computer that will let you manipulate your images; this includes getting rid of red-eye, cutting out unwanted background, darkening or lightening photos, etc. Check your local computer store for such a program, maybe read some online software reviews, and even take a class if you need to. This software is not a necessity, but you can get a more professional look by cleaning up your photos for use in your quilt.

A flat-bed copier/scanner/printer is great for working with photos. If you have a photo that is not already on the computer (transferred from your camera or downloaded), you can scan the image into the computer for clean up and print out.

If an image or writing on a document is too light to make a good copy, the lighter/darker setting on the printer can be changed to several settings darker for a better print.

The images that transfer best are clear ones with high contrast and bright colors. This is not to say that black-and-white photos do not transfer and work well; they do. If you look at an old black-and-white photo, you will find that it is not really true black and white but brown and off-white. If you want this same old photo look, copy it onto the fabric using the color setting. You will get a truer copy of the original with its sepia (brown) tones.

Printing Words and Pictures Directly Onto Fabric

You can print the words you would like to use directly onto the fabric by using the computer and printer. If printing directly to fabric, the words will be in the same order as they are on the computer screen. The reason I mention this here is that the words will be in *reverse* if using the Heat Transfer method as in the following instruction.

The fabric you are printing onto *will need to be treated with a solution that makes the inkjet ink permanent* on the fabric. If the fabric is not treated, the inks will wash away. (This kind of printing onto fabric *cannot* be done with a laser printer.)

There is a product you can purchase to treat the fabric yourself called Bubble Jet Set 2000. The instructions will be included with the purchase. If you want to do this technique, you will need to iron Reynolds brand freezer paper (purchased at the grocery store) to the back of the treated fabric, cut it the size of a sheet of printer paper, trim off all loose threads, and then send it through the printer. The paper will be removed and, after the print has dried for at least thirty minutes, the image will need to be rinsed to remove any excess ink from the surface.

If you prefer to purchase fabric already treated with the solution, there are a couple I recommend for colorfast printing of words and photos: Printed Treasures by Milliken and Sew-in Colorfast Fabric Sheets for Ink Jet Printers by June Tailor, Inc.

Transferring Handwritten Words to Your Quilt

Several different methods can be used to get words onto your fabrics. Words can be hand-colored onto fabric using permanent markers, and they also can be printed directly onto fabric. If printing the words directly onto fabric, there are several important steps you need to follow.

You want the fabric to be a white or a light color and 100 percent cotton or poly−cotton blend with a tight weave. To make the fabric as taut as possible so the pen strokes will flow easily and smoothly, iron Reynold's Freezer Paper (purchased at the grocery store) onto the fabric, placing the wax side against the back side of the fabric. It takes very little time, two to three seconds, and just a medium/hot iron temperature to adhere the freezer paper to the back of the fabric.

If you choose to handwrite words on your quilt, you can do it by tracing. Type the words on your computer and then change the font style. Choose between fancy letters or very simple straight letters that look like handwriting or printing. Change the font size to the one you want for the quilt and print the words out on regular paper. This can then be used for tracing the letters and words onto the fabric.

The best type of pen for this technique is one of the permanent ink pens made for writing on fabrics. Quilters tend to choose Pigma Micron pens by Sakura Color Corporation, which come in a variety of colors and can be purchased at your craft or fabric store. They have a permanent ink and a very small point so you can get a lot of detail with very narrow lines without the ink running and blurring the image.

PHOTO BY *Willow Bodman.*

Words from "The Greatest Moments of a Girl's Life." Illustrations by Harrison Fisher inspired me to make this quilt. I hand-inked words using Pigma Micron pens to explain the meaning of the pictures in the quilt. You can use this hand-inked technique to put words and phrases onto your quilt. Quilt by Linda Pool.

Place the paper with your printed words under the paper-backed fabric and trace the outline of the letters onto the fabric. If you can't see the printed words, tape these layers on a light box or window glass, where the light comes through from the back of the paper. After you trace the outline of the letters, fill in the letters with the Pigma pen. Do this on a flat surface.

The Pigma pens come in several different tip sizes. Number 01 is very small. Number 05 is a little bigger, so you may want the number 05. The tip of the pen also comes in a brush form. This may not be the best tip for making the outline of the letters but could be used for filling in the letters.

After the ink is dry, remove the freezer paper from the back of your inked fabric and press the fabric on both sides with a hot iron. This helps "set" the ink in the fabric. The fabric should be able to be washed without any of the ink washing away. If the ink fades or washes away, the ink you used was not permanent and will not last in your quilt.

Heat-Transfer Your Words or Images onto Fabric

If you would like to use the heat transfer process for your words and photos, you can pick up heat transfer paper at your local office supply store. This is one of my favorite techniques, because you can do so much with it. All you need to transfer the image is your fabric, a photo copied onto heat transfer paper, an iron, and a flat ironing surface. The brand of heat transfer paper is not an issue, as all brands seem to have consistent quality in recent years. Photos on pages 100–101, 130–136, and 144 were made using this heat transfer method.

You can even get a transfer paper that will make your image show up on dark fabric. This is a slightly different process, but the instructions are included.

If printing words, you will need to print them in reverse by using a Transfer or Mirror Image setting on your printer. When you iron the image on the fabric, it will be the reverse of what is printed on the surface of the transfer paper.

For a permanent way to save your children's drawings, you can get them to draw directly onto the transfer paper with markers and then iron this drawing onto fabric. The drawing will be in reverse. However, this will not matter if words, letters, and numbers are not included.

PHOTO BY *Willow Bodman*.

Children's drawings of family memories, 18″ × 28″.
Elementary school students drew these images on
heat transfer paper. Because they used words and
letters in their drawings, I color-copied the images
onto pre-treated fabric, as the letters and words
would have been backwards after ironing them onto
fabric. Quilt by Linda Pool.

Family Stories on Fabric

Showcase a child's drawing on a quilt or tote bag to highlight a family story, an idea, or an inspiration. Teachers and parents can do this project with a child or group of children. Ask the child to draw an image on heat transfer paper using magic markers. The surface of the transfer paper melts when heated by the iron, transferring the drawing onto fabric. No erasing can be done.

When the image is transferred it will be in reverse, so keep this in mind when planning the drawing. Have the child write about the drawing and put the words onto fabric. Stitch them onto the finished quilt or tote bag. This is a child's graphic-inspired memoir.

When using the transfer paper, you can cut any part of the transferred photo away before you iron it onto fabric. You can cut the photo into the shape of a heart, or use your zigzag scrapbooking scissors and add a decorative edge. This edge will transfer as well. You can group photos and cut away any parts that overlap each other, or cut a person out of the photo and transfer that person's image without the background.

Whether you are printing directly onto pre-treated fabric, ironing an image to fabric using heat transfers, or writing words onto fabric with permanent markers, your quilt will still be washable. However, I recommend delicate washing by hand to

PHOTO BY *Willow Bodman.*

Fancy cut image. When using the heat transfer technique to put photos onto fabric, manipulate the image before you iron it onto the fabric for a quilt. For example, use decorative scrapbooking scissors to make fancy edges around the image. Cut away parts of the images that you do not want on the quilt, or change their size and shape to fit odd spaces.

save the beauty and integrity of your transferred images and to ensure a long life for your heirloom memoir quilt.

Have fun and many happy memories!

Signing Your Quilt

A quilt can be a life-long treasure as well as a family heirloom and will be more meaningful to its owner if he or she knows the piece's history. If you are the maker, type a label of information about yourself and the quilt on your computer. Add a photo and then print this onto pre-treated fabric for permanency. Stitch this fabric signature block to the back of your quilt so future generations will know who made the quilt, for whom it was made, where you lived, and any other pertinent information you would like to share. A quilt with a documented history is always more valuable and will be treasured by anyone who owns it.

Designed and Drawn By: Linda Pool
Quilt Made By: Linda Marie (Leaman) Pool
Hand Appliquéd and Hand Quilted
Date Made: August 2012 to January 2014
Where Made: Fredericksburg, Virginia
Inspiration: Scherenschnitte, paper cutting designs
   "When the quilt front appliqué was finished, I just wasn't finished with appliquéing this piece. I enjoyed it so much that I designed the back appliqué to fit the space where the front's appliqué stopped. As I was finishing the appliqué on the quilt's sleeve, I still felt as if I wanted to keep appliquéing. I just love this technique!" Linda Pool

PHOTO BY *Willow Bodman.*

Signature Block from quilt back. The information you want to share about the maker of a quilt can be typed on your computer. Add a photo, print onto pre-treated fabric for permanency, then stitch the block to the back of your quilt. This signature block was made to be stitched to the back of my most recent quilt. Signature Block by Linda Pool.

145

Keep in Mind

- Memoir quilts are usually made to preserve family history, to memorialize a loved one, or to heal a loss and/or recover from a traumatic event.

- Memorable moments are good starting places for creating a quilt that tells a story. Memories to cherish can come from all kinds of experiences: holidays, weddings, pets, hobbies, travel, careers, and so much more. "Memorial" quilts need not be only about death and loss; they can be about relevant happenings in a memorialized one's life: a celebration, a collection, an event, or a representation of the loved one.

- Of all the inspirations for memoir quilts, the challenge is to choose just one subject or idea, one person, or one family as the theme and focal point for your quilt.

- Memoir quilts can be made with more than purchased fabrics; they can include clothing, photos, words, documents, correspondence, and trinkets. Using such well-chosen artifacts triggers memories, helps tell your stories, and helps you make a connection to the past.

- Images can be added to memoir quilts in three ways: copying directly to the fabric, hand-lettering, or converting your image to a heat transfer, and ironing it onto fabric.

- Ensure a long life for your heirloom memoir quilt by delicate hand-washing and proper fabric care.

Chapter 7
NURTURING THE YOUNG STORYTELLER

— *By Nadine Majette James* —

Listen—your child is reliving the moment, retelling an event from his or her own unique perspective. Nothing could be more valuable than capturing those moments! After all, crafting a memoir is not just for adults.

This chapter explores memoirs from a younger writer's point of view, as well as how crafting a memoir can preserve childhood's most precious times. It provides tips for introducing children to the craft of memoir and encouraging them as they gain confidence and comfort with self-expression at home and at school. You'll also find ways to involve children in family memoir projects, including grandparent interviews and other age-appropriate activities.

The Foundation for Storytelling Begins When We're Very Young

Your toddler looks on and listens as you talk to your mom in Virginia about how to make her sweet potato pie. She or he sees shapes magically appear as you move the pen or you hit each key and notices that you give each shape a name as you recite your list: *sugar, eggs, milk . . .*

You might not realize it, but even with something as simple as a shopping list, you've already modeled how people express themselves through writing. Add crayons, markers, paint, paper, and photos to the mix, and children are ready to share with you the pictures in their heads.

Often the pictures are about birthdays, outings, and family visits—in other words, they are your child's first memoirs. These self-expressions of a child are fleeting, but you can give them permanence by simply dating them, adding a caption, and saving them in a file or shoe box. Most important, a few words of praise—"Very good. I'm going to save this one for Grandma's birthday card!"—go a long way in helping your child feel confident about storytelling and enthusiastic about memoir projects.

IMAGE BY *Willow Bodman.*

Child's Journal: "The Time I was Most Scared." A fourth-grader recalls a time when he was afraid during a Boy Scout camping trip. His father helped him and other scouts overcome their fears.

To further build your child's confidence and enthusiasm, consider scanning these "first memoirs" into the computer to demonstrate their importance and so that you have them for future memoir projects. Most printers now have a scanning feature. If not, you can scan them at your local drugstore, supply/ copy center, or public library.

Connecting the Dots in the Story

As you know, you are your child's first teacher. When it comes to children creating their own memoirs, they learn patience, creativity, and achievement by watching you put together scrapbooks, lay out and sew your quilts, and protect your favorite handwritten recipes and cookbooks as you gourmet up the kitchen.

When you become a role model by pursuing your own craft and memoir projects, the children in your life not only watch your actions, but they see the *connections* you make between the words, stamps, photos, fabrics, and other ingredients, and the story you are telling. In this way, children understand that this connection is not only to story, but to *their own story*, or identity— the family present and past, the history and culture that helped to create them and helps them know who they are.

Imagine the conversations you could have:

"See this one square in the quilt? It came from your Great-Uncle Will's baseball uniform. We used to call him Lightfoot. I bet you didn't know that he played for the Negro National League in the 1940s."

"Do you believe this photo is your Aunt Dolly? Was she cute or what! You have her green eyes, and she loved rock music as much as you do. Grandad had a fit when she snuck off to go see the Beatles in New York."

"I got this recipe for sweet rolls from Grandma, even though I could never get her to write it down. I had to watch her bake and take notes as best I could. Hand me that . . ."

Fast forward a few years later to your fifth-grader now faced with a rigorous writing assessment test in school: The teacher places an old wooden chest in the center of the classroom. "Your assignment is to create a story explaining where it came from, what it was used for, and who previously owned it. Be creative and include as many details as possible."

Now who's going to ace the test? The children who grew up with story-telling and self-expression, of course! Ideas and memory, descriptions, colors, and textures will flood their brains. Best of all, they will be able to visualize an answer, access those pictures, and express them in words.

So as your child watches and listens to you, so does he build his skills and abilities

It is so important that you *listen* to your child. I'm not recommending you pull off the highway to capture that thirty-four-word garbled blab about the fairy tale–themed birthday party. Still, tuning in and listening to your child's stories and descriptions helps show that his or her point of view and experiences are important to you. That is a real confidence-builder.

With the passing of years, the collected bits of sticky notes and papers filled with your child's words and saved for later, hidden away in a special place, can become a treasure chest of childhood wonder.

In a larger sense, these bits and pieces become part of the family heritage that your child is connected to. Peggy Kaye, author of *Games for Writing*, chronicles that journey in her book. She reminds us how storytelling is the very foundation of learning to express ourselves through writing.

Before we move on to tips and tricks for working with children on memoir projects, here is a short note about reading to them.

Reading Plays a Role

When books are read to children, they hear the words and use their imaginations. Connecting the story to their own lives expands their world. In other words, *"It's not just me that has a scary dream; it's the boy in the story, too!"* Classic fairy tales and folktales endure to this day because of their universality, and they are a gold mine when it comes to reaching children with the joys of reading and storytelling. The excitement children feel for a story they love encourages them to tell their own stories. It's imitation at its best.

Sample Projects and Activities

Here are some activities you can do with children, or set them up to work on independently.

A "My First" Timeline

If your story involves the progression of time, simple timelines can be made by decorating index cards and gluing them to a string to show different important dates. For example, "My First" is a great place to start for a child's timeline: my first steps, my first words, my first day at school.

A timeline can also serve as a memoir project outline, as different old photos or news-clippings are attached to the index cards as a way of organizing them into your memoir.

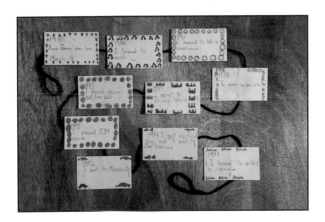 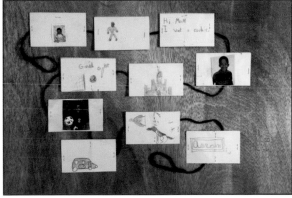

Child's first timeline. Items found around the house such as crayons, index cards, and yarn can be used to chronicle your child's life.

Homemade Family Folktales

A folktale is a story that has been handed down orally through the generations. So why not create family folktales? They can be small, like when the family first came to America's shores. Or they can be big, like when Great-Grandma Jane was arrested in Virginia in 1961 during segregation for refusing to move herself and her pupils to the back of the bus on a field trip. What happened as a result? Who bailed her out? What happens when the story is retold and embellished? These are the ingredients for great family folktales.

Nothing's better than a homemade family storybook, because the ingredients are homegrown. Your child recognizes the characters, the setting, and the emotions. When you and your child together put these elements in the form of a book or memory project (calendar, scrapbook, cookbook, voice recording, etc.), your child's self-esteem and family connections grow. And most importantly, it's fun!

IMAGE BY *Willow Bodman.*

Family folktale book: "The Wonderful Marvelous Incredibly Radical Totally Awesome Day." A favorite storybook inspires a young storyteller's imaginative tale.

Family Newspapers

This kind of project is good for ages seven and up. If you are working with younger children, let them help you.

A family newspaper is a good project to do on your computer. It also lends itself beautifully to a family event such as a wedding, reunion, or holiday. The trick to creating a family newspaper is using all the elements of a regular newspaper, such as a front-page banner with the newspaper name, front-page headlines, and so on.

Let your child be the editor-in-chief and relate things from his or her point of view. If you have a group, each person can be "delegated a news beat" and contribute one piece for the paper. Here are some suggestions for getting started:

1. Create a lead story. What happened?

2. Add a drawing, photos, and even a cartoon.

3. Add some human interest stories (like the role your child played at the wedding—was she the flower girl?).

4. Add a funny human interest story, e.g., Cousin Jay ate too much cake and threw up.

5. Believe it or not, children love survey questions. Let them pick a question, such as "What was your favorite part of the wedding—the ceremony or the reception, or both?" They will "survey" a couple of family members and put the results in the paper.

6. Older children can even do a one-paragraph opinion editorial (an "op-ed")—their own take on the event.

Holiday Newsletters

If you enjoy sending out an annual holiday letter to family and friends, consider having your child write and illustrate part of the letter. It means so much to family that's far away, and it helps the child reflect on the past year and goals for the year ahead.

Helping Children Interview Family Members

Back in the early years of my teaching career, I invited my second-graders to celebrate Grandparents Day by becoming involved in a special project called "My Grandparent Remembers." As part of the activity, I hoped to expand my students' understanding of their own history and heritage by having them ask family members a broad range of questions with a slight twist. All the questions began with "when you were my age."

One day my students were sharing their interview videos in class. In one video, a little boy asked his grandfather, "When you were my age, what was your favorite song?" Without hesitation, his grandfather burst into a song from his own childhood. I maintained my composure, but inside I was simultaneously laughing and crying for many reasons. I thought about the many memories these interviews had captured, and all the families that would be forever changed in the process. I was convinced that the "interview" is the key to family memoir. The interview transformed a simple school project into a great story.

The children loved doing these projects and remembered them as they grew older. I was lucky enough to hear from one of my former second-graders whom I had encouraged as a storyteller. She said her family still had her grandparent interview. Years later, one of her stories was published in the Scholastic book, *The Best Teen Writing of 2012*. In the copy she gave me, her inscription read, "Thank you so much for your work as my teacher helping me along my way to becoming a writer."

When you begin a memoir project with a child, you know you're going to have fun, but where those storytelling moments will take you in the future can be more than you or your child can foresee in the present moment. The project could be the beginning of something that neither of you has imagined.

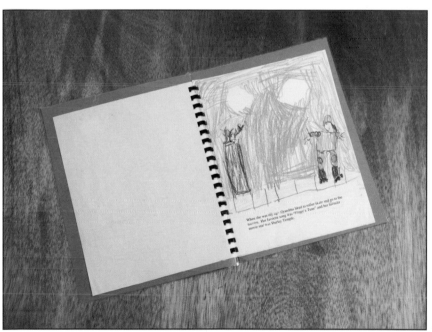

IMAGE BY *Willow Bodman.*

"My Grandparent Remembers." Second-grader Emma illustrated her grandparent interview book. She interviewed her "mom's mom."

Interviewing is important to creating family memoir projects because it supplies the details: day-to-day activities, special events, and what loved ones thought about them. Your child will ask open-ended questions and find out what Grandma and Grandpa saw, thought, dreamed, and feared. Hearing the responses allows your child to step back into history, to walk in a grandparent's footsteps—better yet, to walk with the grandparent, while recording unique stories that cannot be gathered by *any other method* of historical documentation.

You might think that our senior relatives have better things to do than to answer questions about themselves, but think again. Just about everybody loves that type of attention. Plus, they might be so surprised that the young people are interested in their life experiences that they'll spend quite a bit of time coming up with answers.

Create a Questionnaire—Good Questions Make All the Difference

The purpose of the interview questions is to create a path for the story. Questions guide the discussion and keep things on track, ensuring that basic but oh-so-precious information will be covered. Remember that young children might need several sessions to complete an interview with a family member. Record each interviewing session in the way that works for you: taking notes by hand, typing into a computer, or using a voice or video recorder.

Help children develop questions that cover a range of events and include a balance of "factual" and reflective questions. You might want to send the interviewee a list of suggested questions from which he or she may choose. However, certain information should be gathered consistently, such as the interviewee's date and place of birth. Beginning with questions about early childhood remembrances taps stronger memories and allows the interviewee to become more reflective. I have also observed that as interviewees answer the questions, a strong bond is created between the interviewer and the interviewee, and both are happy that they have created this bit of history for the next generation. You'll be amazed by how seriously children take their job of interviewing grandparents and family. They really get into it!

Questions Appropriate for Elementary-Age Interviewers

- What was your name at birth? (Ask about nicknames)

- Where were you born?

- What was the date of your birth?

- How much did the following cost when you were my age?
  - Gasoline per gallon
  - Postage stamp
  - A soft drink
  - A candy bar

- When you were my age, what or who was your favorite?
  - Sports star
  - Song
  - Movie star
  - School subject

- What was school like when you were my age?

- What did you like best/hate most about school?

- What time did you have to go to bed on a school night?

- What were your chores at home?

- What was the fashion when you were my age? What did you wear to school?

Image by Willow Bodman.

"My Grandfather Makes History." Later, as a middle school student, Emma wrote an essay about her paternal grandfather's participation in a flying mission during World War II. He was the radio man on the bomber Lucky. Her father told her that her grandfather, along with the rest of the crew, received a Distinguished Flying Cross, which at the time was the highest award given to an airman. Emma's riveting essay was saved for all to read.

Questions Middle or High School Students Might Ask:

- Describe your family, including the role of your mother and father in the household and their occupations.

- Describe your family life and your daily life.

- Describe your school, friends, hobbies, and organizations.

- What were your family's political or religious affiliations?

- What are your recollections of the town or city where you were born?

- How did you get your job?

- Describe any cultural, social, or religious activities: concerts, lectures, parties, religious observances.

- Were the lives of women and men different or similar when you were growing up?

- When were you considered a "grown-up"? How is that different from or similar to what we consider "grown-up" today?

Conducting an interview takes children beyond their own world. For example, ask children what they know about history and the response may often be, "I don't know." The concept of "family history" might be abstract to them with little or no connection to their own lives. When they interview family members, children learn that people are "History!" Furthermore, by the end of the interviews, grandparents or senior family members perceived as ordinary old people will indeed be recognized for the awesome people they are. Their lives are indeed remarkable. The time spent organizing and arranging an interview for your child is well worth it!

What Is Age-Appropriate?

Keep in mind the age of your storyteller when starting a project. Here are some guidelines:

Ages 0–3: Read to them. Yes, even when they are babies, before they can talk. Hearing stories creates the fertile soil from which a child's own stories will someday take root.

Ages 4–6: Let them *help you* create a family memoir project. Include their words, photos, and drawings. This is when role-modeling and enthusiasm are so important. For example, "Let's write a story for the photos!" or "Help me decorate Grandma's cookbook. Will you draw a picture for it?"

Ages 7 on up: You'll need to set up your child with materials, including computer software if he or she is working digitally. Take a few minutes to talk with your child to create the plan or outline for the project. From there, you take on the role of supporter. Remember that your child might not be able to finish it in one sitting (very few do). You might take what they do accomplish and include it as part of the family memoir.

Children will often write down what people say—or what they *think* people might have said. These inventions, too, are a precious part of children's storytelling. So even though your child wasn't there when relatives from Vietnam were rescued to begin a new life in America, and no one ever said, "Welcome to America. Land of the free and home of the brave," please consider leaving it as is, and don't discourage your child from putting his or her own words into characters' mouths. It's part of your child's enthusiastic storytelling and perspective. Getting to share is what it's all about.

The Ripple Effect of Connections

One of the gifts of working with children is that it supports your own projects about your own childhood. Their drawings and words will trigger your own memories of being little, which will re-ignite memories such as the bad taste of old-fashioned medicine, falling asleep in your mom's lap, or the sounds of city life around your apartment building. All of these triggers will allow your own stories to come forward more clearly.

Keep in Mind

- The foundation for storytelling begins at a very young age as your child listens to you.
- Simple arts and crafts, and talking and *listening* to your children, can build their skills and self-esteem.
- Write down children's stories and what they say for use in a childhood memoir project later on.

- Read storybooks and folktales to children to expand their world through the universality of emotions and themes.
- Family stories can be turned into precious homemade family folktales.
- Include your child in your own memoir activities.
- Interviewing family members is a process of joy and discovery for children; help them create a questionnaire that's age-appropriate.

Chapter 8

YOU ARE THE BRIDGE: TRADITIONS AND HERITAGE

— *By Dianne Hennessy King* —

Who am I? Who were the people in my family

who came before me? What made them laugh,

what made them strong, whom did they love?

Maybe you're lucky enough to know something about your heritage, maybe not. No matter how familiar you are with parts of your family history, there's always hope of finding out a little bit more to have a clearer idea of what made your relatives real.

Credit: Hennessy family photo.

Great-Grandparents. Those who came before us are so much of who we are today.

This chapter shows how to explore more of your heritage in areas such as cultural history, music, dance, food, and holidays. You can choose which traditions to include in your life today and pass them on to the next generation.

Rudyard Kipling said, "If history were taught in the form of stories, it would never be forgotten." Remember that memoir is simply telling your story. Decide which facts you want to include. Did your family dance the polka or bhangra? Did they eat tamales for Christmas or harira soup for Eid al Adha? Did they listen to folktales told by griots or lullabies sung by grandmothers? Did they come to the United States recently or have they been here since the 1700s or earlier? What's your story?

Those who came before us are so much of who we are today. We don't just carry their genes—we carry their stories as we create our daily lives. If we don't remember their stories, who will? If we don't tell their stories, how will they live on in history?

Where to Start

Many people think of family history as tracing roots back hundreds of years, which can sound like a lot of work. The internet, though, has made everything so much easier. You don't have to travel to some distant courthouse to look through birth records, and you don't have to wait weeks for letters to travel back and forth to a grandfather in Indonesia or a second cousin in Estonia. You can find out much of what you want in the comfort of your own home with a computer, tablet, or smartphone. How far back do you have to go? Not far. You might be happy looking back at the last hundred years or so—it's completely up to you.

Start with the people you know. Your family elders are your living history, able to tell you about life for part of the last century. If you want to learn more, this chapter will point you to some resources to help you find additional information about your family.

Knowing the names and birthdates of your grandparents or great-grandparents doesn't mean you know how they lived or what their world was like. You have to look at a few other things to see a fuller picture.

Where to Look

Public records and documents that flesh out unknown parts of your family history are available for the asking—if you know where to look. Finding your family history can be like solving a mystery or puzzle. When researching your family's history, consider looking at the clues found in genealogy, geography, politics, and cultural history.

Genealogy

Genealogy has become a passion for millions of people. Many of us never had the spare time to conduct research—or the talkative relatives to fill in the details. But now so many public records—birth, marriage, death, military,

Credit: Ruth Bennett.

Char McCargo Bah and Dianne Hennessy King in television interview about African American genealogy. The search for family is a passion for millions of people.

immigration, migration, and census—are online. These government documents are increasingly digitized and are usually free.

Start with the National Archives and the Library of Congress, both of which have directions on their home pages for using their collections for family history research. For example, if you've heard stories that a long-ago relative named John O'Brien came over from Ireland because times were bad there, you might start your research in the National Archives' Genealogy section by looking at the "Passenger lists of boats into the Ports of New York City 1846–51" or "Famine Irish data files."

The Library of Congress is a treasure trove of thousands of photos, exhibits, and special studies such as "America Eats," a collection of images of people eating and cooking at social gatherings in the 1930s. The "America Eats" study was produced by special initiatives such as the Federal Writers' Project, which hired writers, artists, and photographers to create WPA State Travel Guides for each of the (then) forty-eight states.

Whether you're researching land records, immigration records, or special-interest topics like African American heritage or Chinese immigration, you are almost guaranteed to find information at these two government organizations.

Don't overlook state historical societies and readily available local resources. One of my students who grew up above her family's small grocery shop in the Bronx went to the New York City Historical Society and found a photograph of her parents' store from the late 1930s. Another student was amazed to find that her 450-person hometown in the Midwest now has a website collection of maps; photos of schools, places of worship, and main streets; and old newspapers and telephone books that contain residents' names and addresses, as well as business advertisements. If you can't remember the name of the local drugstore or restaurant you used to visit when you were five years old, you might be able to find it on your hometown's website. In addition, countries around the world are gradually going online with their public records, making it much easier to find branches on your family tree.

Geography and Economics

Researching your family history doesn't necessarily end with knowing what country your relatives came from. It's also fascinating to learn where

Credit: *Minnesota Timber Association.*

A logging camp in Minnesota. Look for information on where and how your ancestors earned their living.

and why they moved around the United States or why they decided to stay put in one area. At the beginning of your research, your family history can be one big mystery. But, you can solve it! Knowing something about your ancestors' occupations and where they might have lived can speed up your research by narrowing where you need to look for information.

In the United States, people frequently moved in search of better farm land, forests, and pastures. If your ancestor was an immigrant logger in the late 1800s, for example, he was more likely to head for places like forested Idaho or northern Minnesota. In 1900 more than half of the US population was employed in farm-related work. If your ancestor tried farming in the rocky spots of Vermont, her family might have made tracks for western regions where the soil was deeper and darker.

Natural disasters also motivated rural people to leave farming or small-town life and move to large cities, other regions of the country, or even to other countries. In Ireland, the Potato Famine of 1845–1852 drove about a million people out of the country, and many immigrated to new lives and jobs in American cities.

The Dust Bowl in the United States, caused by drought and poor farming practices, resulted in three-and-a-half million people leaving the Plains states between 1930 and 1940, desperate to find a better life. When you learn even a little about where your ancestors were born, or where they moved and how they earned their living, you gain a better understanding of their lives and challenges.

Politics

The politics of war, religious differences, rulers, and shifting country borders all influenced those who came to the United States. Once upon a time, for example, Puritans on the Mayflower were escaping religious persecution and political oppression—and this emigration ultimately led to George Washington crossing the Delaware to fight a tyrant. Each century has many examples of political upheaval. Within the last fifty years, the United States has welcomed refugees from areas in turmoil such as Cuba, Vietnam, North Africa, and Central America, to name only a few examples. Global political conditions still contribute to the ebb and flow of culture all over the world. Again, it's easier to trace your lineage if you have some clues as to the dates and kinds of upheavals that were going on in the part of the world where your family originated.

Cultural History

Cultural history includes looking at holidays, food traditions, oral history, folklore, art, music, dance, and other traditions that your family celebrates. These traditions are often the easiest ways to share your heritage with children.

Holidays

What holidays did your family celebrate in the past? Today, in a three-week period, millions of people might celebrate Christmas, Boxing Day, Kwanzaa, Hanukkah, Epiphany, and the New Year, among other holidays. On New Year's Eve do you wear red underwear, make sure your house is clean, or eat twelve grapes, one for each month's good luck in the next year? Does your family celebrate a New Year such as Chinese or Persian that follows the lunar calendar? Pick any month and you'll find holidays that your family might have celebrated, such as Diwali in November or a harvest festival in October.

What holidays do you celebrate?

Food Traditions

What's not to love about finding the best cake in your family's recipe collection? Or sampling the main dish that brought your family members comfort after they left their country and moved to a strange place? Check out the "Around the Table: Food and Cookbook Memoirs" chapter for questions to ask about the foods your family savored. Pick your pleasure and pass it on.

Oral History, Folklore, and Art

Much of what we know about our family is passed down to us in family stories told by a parent, aunt, or someone else in our family. For many cultures, that's the only way history has been kept. You can keep the oral tradition alive by making a video or a recording of a family member telling the stories you have heard since childhood. Oral history blends with folklore, which consists of the stories that folks hand down, sometimes orally, sometimes in writing, and sometimes through art. If, for example, you want to find out more about German fairy tales, Navajo kachina dolls, or stories your family would have told about their heroes (George Washington and the cherry tree?), you could look to folklore. The Library of Congress houses the American Folklife Center, which is the home of thousands and thousands of files of information on folklore and folklife.

The Smithsonian Institution in Washington D.C. also has a wonderful folklife center and a folk music catalogue, all available online. And each summer the Smithsonian Institution puts on a terrific Folklife Festival that features the music, art, traditional skills, and storytellers from one American state and usually one or two countries. Most of the presentations on everything from building a canoe to making maple syrup to regional dances are stored on the Smithsonian's website.

We often look to art to show us the stories of our heritage. For example, beginning with the Federal Arts Program, photographers like Berenice Abbott and painters like Thomas Hart Benton and Jacob Lawrence documented our history in the 1930s and 1940s and beyond. Today, newspaper photographers and documentary filmmakers use their artistic vision to record the lives of communities near and far from us. Both modern and traditional artists of all genres continue to open our eyes to the beauty and diversity of cultures everywhere.

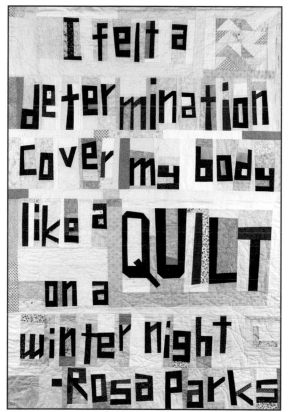

PHOTO BY *Donna Callighan's* Photo Designs.

The words of Rosa Parks were put onto a quilt titled "Determination," made by artist Christina Blais. Artists help us see the world through many lenses. Quilt by Christina Blais.

Music and Dance

Music and dance are international languages with almost no political boundaries. Each culture celebrates its own favorite rhythms of music and dance. See if you can find out what music your parents or grandparents listened to and danced to; it's fun research, and you'll get to know your relatives better by experiencing what they enjoyed.

Children today start making playlists at a fairly early age. Why not add a "heritage" playlist to the family's music collection? Your family's favorite music might have been jazz, country, blues, classical, hip hop, gospel, or global—it's all available to discover and enjoy. Music and dance videos are everywhere on the internet. Name almost any dance your family loved and you probably can find a video showing you the steps; name an old song and you often can listen to someone singing it online. Now you've found another way to connect your present and future to your past.

We also can share our current favorite music with friends and family. Friends of mine gave their wedding guests a CD of the music they gave to each other while they were dating. Side one contained her favorite songs, side two contained his. I love playing their celebration music. It reminds me of the joy of treasuring memories while looking forward to the future.

You Are the Bridge

Let us not forget that, as we honor our ancestors' stories, we need to record and celebrate the stories of our own lives. Our lives also are worth remembering and sharing with the next generation. Today is tomorrow's history.

Keep in Mind

- Researching your family history can start simply: ask family elders for family stories.

- Use the internet to find historical records, information from ethnic and social affinity groups, and public records that can fill in the facts behind family stories.

- A family's traditions of food, music, dance, literature, and folktales provide insight into its cultural heritage.

- Once you know more about your heritage, choose the ways you want to preserve those stories, whether through cooking, keeping a scrapbook or journal, making a quilt, writing or drawing a story, or some other way that makes you happy.

- Find ways to enjoy now what your ancestors enjoyed then: sports, music, food, dance, and art—name your passion.

Don't stop there. Remember to tell the stories of your own life. Pass on the stories to the next generation. Don't you wish someone had done that for you?

Appendix A
GETTING OVER YOUR FEAR OF WRITING

— *By Joanne Lozar Glenn* —

You have a story that's just itching to get out into the world. Still, you keep thinking about the teacher who said you couldn't write or the one who punished you for daydreaming.

Any memoir project—cookbooks, scrapbooks, even quilts—will probably involve at least some writing, to set the stage for story. And some memoir projects, such as photo essays (photos arranged in sequence, sometimes accompanied by captions that help tell the story) or books, will use writing as the main vehicle for telling the tale.

Trouble is, many of us don't feel confident about our writing, so we face a lot of obstacles when beginning this type of project. You might think, for instance, that your life isn't interesting enough, or that you don't have that much to say. You might worry about having enough time to do a good job, or that your writing isn't strong enough, or even that you'll end up doing this "wrong."

This appendix is about overcoming those obstacles. Whether you've been criticized for how you told stories, or had teachers "bleed" all over your compositions with a red pen, know this: there is no wrong way to tell your story.

Here are some tools for jumpstarting your memoir project, plus inspiration for finding your natural voice as a writer—and letting it sing.

There Is No Wrong Way to Tell Your Story

If you're reading this book, you know that there are multiple ways to craft a memoir: scrapbooks and photo essays, food and cookbook memoirs, memory quilts, videotaped interviews. Likewise, there's no wrong way to do the writing (or voice-overs, if you're videotaping the stories) that goes along with some of these memoir projects.

Just get the story down. Pretend you're talking to a friend over coffee, or to your sister when you're clearing the table, or to your kids when you're reminiscing about the good old days.

You Have a Natural Writing Voice

Your writing voice is your personality coming out on paper. The key is to sound like yourself. Don't try too hard. Don't worry about spelling or punctuation, especially not when you're writing the story for the first time. You can always change things later.

Follow the action—write down what happened. Let us see what you saw, hear what you heard, experience what you smelled, tasted, touched. As Kevin Boggs, a storyteller from Arlington, Virginia, says, "Your one single voice, being vulnerable and true, [is] enough to tell a story that makes an impact on your audience."

You'll Always Have Something to Say

Have you ever tried to think of nothing? It's near-impossible. Your brain processes 12,000 to 70,000 thoughts each day. In fact, Cary Tennis, who writes for *Salon* magazine, shared a great writing exercise based on this very notion of how hard it is to think of nothing. I invite you to try it. Ready?

Get whatever you need to write—computer or pen and paper. Set a timer for seven to ten minutes. Start with this sentence—*Every time I try to sit and think of nothing, this is what I see . . .* —and write until the timer goes off.

You will be amazed at what comes up. Congratulations! You've written a mini-memoir.

You Can Write Something Meaningful Even If You Have "No Time"

If you did the previous exercise, you've just proven you don't need long blocks of time to write something meaningful. Some of the best writing I've seen comes from writing against the clock. Why? Because racing to tell a story in five, seven, or ten minutes sharpens your focus. That laser-like focus shuts down the Censor—aka the ghost of the teacher who red-penned all your assignments.

Shutting down the Censor allows your brain to pull from the Unconscious, the "artist" part of your brain that makes patterns out of details you thought you'd forgotten, and serves them up "whole." When you read what you wrote, you'll feel that the story has come "full circle." It's a byproduct of being human. We humans are pattern-making creatures. When we get out of our own way, we can write stories that can stun our readers and ourselves.

The story below was written in about seven minutes, in response to the word "Advice":

Mother was right! I didn't think so when I was young. Now that I'm older, I know that in spite of her lack of formal education, she had wisdom.

"Don't eat so much candy! You'll wear your body out and get diabetes." Check! I'm diabetic type II.

"Stand up straight." Check! Probably I'd have less back and neck problems if I'd done so.

"He's not the marrying kind," she said of my young adult boyfriend. Check! One evening, somehow I just knew that was the last I'd see of him. Not a word of explanation but true.

"You're lazy, Joan." Now I don't think I was then, but those words echo in my mind as I sit in my Lazy Boy chair and read the papers or watch television.

How did she come to knowing these things? She used to say, "I graduated from the college of hard knocks." Probably so! As I look back at her life, I see she had quite a struggle to become the person she was. And become she did.

—Joan Carr, 5/26/11

Your Life IS Interesting

Do you know what makes it so? The concrete details. The sights, sounds, tastes, textures, and smells that are part of any memory. The more specific the writing gets, the more interesting it becomes.

Let me say it again. The more specific you get about even the small, ordinary moments that make up the part of your life you want to write about, the more your story comes alive. And the truer your voice, the more moving your story.

So include the details about the machinist oil on the front of the Hanes T-shirt your father wore when he watered the lettuce and cucumber vines with a garden hose that arced like a snake, or the way your mother's Maybellined eyebrows looked like big parentheses that had fallen sideways over her eyes and how her fingers, marked by cuts from potato peelers and paring knives, still reached for your father's hand when they walked to the glider in the backyard. Moments make up a life, and these kinds of details capture the moments in a way that holds your audience's attention.

Now, Jumpstart Your Memoir Project

Keep reading for some can't-miss tools to get you started.

Lists

Make a list of your memories. The next time you face a blank page (or computer screen), pick something from your list and write about it.

Your list can center on a theme, like growing up on a farm or as an Army brat, or leaving one country to live in another; working as a firefighter, a nurse, a policeman; or maybe being the first person in your extended family to attend college. Or your list can be full of random recollections that seem particularly vivid to you—things you can't forget. Hint: You don't have to list everything. In fact, you shouldn't. That could get tedious.

Stick with the memories you think of often, or the memories that surprise you by appearing out of nowhere, or the times, big and small, that were turning points for you. These memories are usually significant touch points, and probably rich with the detail that will let your audience understand what your life was truly like.

Objects

It's been said that objects—the gold bracelet your mother gave you, the thimble your grandfather the tailor used to sew buttons on shirts—bring us the world. The objects of our lives are rich with meaning. You can use objects to release memories that give snapshots of your life, preserved in writing, for those you care about.

The beauty of using objects as writing triggers is that often you will discover things you never knew you knew. Discovery is what gives your writing "juice." As Rebecca McClanahan, who wrote movingly in *The Riddle Song* about being the younger sister of a baby who had died at birth, tells us, "Memory is not the same as recalling information. Memory—memoir—is the art of meaning-making."

That's really what your children and their children want to know about you and your life. Not just what you did or had, but what it meant to you. Not just what you looked like or whom and what you loved, but what that says about who you are, deep inside.

Maps

Ralph Fletcher, who's written a beautifully simple book called *How to Write Your Life Story,* suggests starting a memoir by drawing a map of the neighborhood where you grew up. You just close your eyes and picture the place as it used to be: the trees that were home base when you played "Olley Olley In Free," the houses where your friends lived, the stores and bars around the corner, the gardens and the fields, the ladders stowed on the dirt floor of the garage—whatever comes to mind. Then take unlined paper and some crayons or markers and start drawing.

When Fletcher did this, he surprised himself. The more he drew, the more details he added; the more details he added, the more he remembered. He began to label specific places on the map, marking where something had happened to him (like losing a tooth), a "power spot" (where all the kids gathered), a "danger spot" (that he had avoided), a favorite place, and a secret place.

"Instead of a treasure map, you are making a 'story map' and it's very helpful," he says. "Many important stories are rooted in the important places in our lives."

Fletcher also suggests making a "heart map," an idea he got from poet and teacher Georgia Heard. A heart map is like a map of your neighborhood, but "with a twist—it's an emotional map of what matters to you." A heart map is a great way to identify important events and memories—for example, the time your family moved and you had to change schools, the time you received a gift you didn't want, or the chocolate-covered cherries your spouse gives you each year for your birthday. These are also rich sources of story.

This excerpt from a memoir called "A Morning in Durg" is both a story map and a heart map. It was written by a woman who grew up in India and shows an important memory, set in a faraway time and place, about how her father ("Pitaji") taught her to tell time:

The solitary clock in the house hangs above the fireplace in the dining room, ticking time with its pendulum swinging back and forth, back and forth, dependent on the servant winding it once every twenty-four hours.

"Let me show you an easier way," Pitaji says. "And this clock never requires winding or servicing. It travels with you wherever you go."

My eyes brighten.

Pitaji buries the tip of his walking stick in a natural crack in the dry barren ground, and steadies it upright by stamping down some dusty red gravel around it. By now, the big bright ball [of the sun] has risen above the eastern horizon. The stick makes a thin pencil-like shadow. Using the length of the shadow as a radius, he draws a perfect circle around the stick [and] . . . a straight line across the diameter of the circle, tracing the line of the shadow, going past the base of the stick and continuing to the other side.

"This is the line that the shadow will traverse through the course of the day as the sun travels east to west from sunrise to sunset," he explains. "Now fetch some stones."

I walk around the compound, still chewing and spitting [the carved neem branch that serves as toothbrush and toothpaste] and do as I am told. I place five stones on either side of the stick neatly dividing the line into twelve segments, each marking an hour of the twelve-hour day. I am to track the shadow made by the stick through the day, watch it shorten, jumping one stone on the hour every hour and becoming undecipherable at the base of the stick at noon. It will elongate towards the other side in the afternoon and again touch the perimeter of the circle at six in the evening.

I think the sun is very clever and Pitaji a genius.

After a little practice, I am able to tell time to the closest hour by observing the length of the shadow.

"Now that you understand how this works, remember that you don't necessarily need a stick or stones to tell time. Just use your own shadow," Father explains. Our lesson for the day is complete.

—*Urmilla Khanna, 8/2/09*

Photographs

You probably have a bunch of photographs, old and new, tucked away in shoeboxes or computer files. These photos can serve as triggers for writing the stories associated with the photographed event or for describing the family members involved.

Start by selecting one photo that you like. Write about the photo in any way that feels right. For example:

- You can name the people and describe what was happening.

- You can decide to focus on one of the subjects in the photo, starting with the words, "In this one, you . . ." or "If only you . . ." or whatever phrase comes up—in effect, writing *to* the photo.

- Or you can imagine you are speaking *for* the subject in the photo, telling what you imagine he, she, or it (a house maybe?) would say in their own words.

- Another idea is to imagine yourself as the silent, observant camera. What did you see before or after the picture was taken?

Even photos and postcards that are not in any way related to you can be an interesting way to write something about yourself or your family. Lawrence Sutin, a child of parents who survived the Holocaust, uses this approach. He collects antique postcards. He stares at them until their subjects trigger an association in his mind, and then he writes. Surprisingly, or perhaps not (because our brains, remember, are always making patterns from the data that comes to us!), each of the writings revealed stories about his own life or family or people he knew. Eventually he collected all these writings and put them together with images from the triggering postcards in a book he called *A Postcard Memoir*.

I tried his technique with a postcard from friend and writing mentor Pat Schneider's collection. The sepia-toned image showed three men sitting on a bench. One of the men wore a newsboy's cap tilted just so over one eye, and that, combined with his expression, reminded me of my mother's brother. Here's what came out:

"If that don't beat all," I can hear my brother saying, "he's the spitting image of Uncle Sam."

On the Christmas Eves we spent at Grandma's you could count on Sam to argue with the rest of the uncles about everything—the changing neighborhood, how he was neglecting his wife and kids, maybe even his drinking.

The men always stood in the breezeway at the back of the house while the rest of us picked at the relish tray full of olives and pickles, then grabbed a slice of my aunt's strudel and my mother's potica before it was gone. The uncles would swirl the ice in their highballs, lift their cigarettes to their mouths, and tell Sam he was nuts.

As I understand it, Sam is why we have no heirlooms or antiques in our family. He sold or gave away to the church—no one is really sure—Grandma's Singer treadle sewing machine and her lace-covered mahogany sideboard. The rest of it—furniture, clothes, house—all burned down years later when he fell asleep with a lit cigarette, or so the story goes, and died. Being that he was my mother's brother, though, I wouldn't be surprised if it was no accident. His wife and kids were long gone by then, his mother was dead, and the neighborhood had turned. Just one more thing going up in smoke, and maybe, after all was said and done, a blessing for him, and for us.

This kind of exercise can be the start of a memoir project that paints portraits of the relatives in your extended family—as it might be for mine.

Prompts

A writing prompt is something that triggers writing. Technically, all of the above tools—lists, objects, maps, and photographs—can be thought of as prompts. A prompt invites you to write something, but leaves the direction of what you write up to you.

Words can also work as prompts. For example, any of these words—wishbone, Ferris wheel, ghost—could trigger a memory: so can an open-ended sentence like Cary Tennis's *"Every time I close my eyes and try to think of nothing, this is what I see"* or random phrases taken from a newspaper article (put your finger anywhere on the page; use that phrase in your writing). Even lines from a favorite poem or song, or something you overheard in a coffee shop or department store, can trigger a wonderful story about your life.

The beauty of prompts is that (1) they are everywhere; (2) they can be used over and over again with different results each time; and (3) they can surprise you into telling a complete, well-developed story in a really short amount of time, or generating seeds for future writing.

There's no perfect time limit for writing in response to prompts. Spend as little or as much time as you like. When I write from a prompt, I like to limit the time to seven, ten, or fifteen minutes, then race the clock. It helps me get out of my own way and lets the story scroll through my mind like a movie; all I have to do is record what I see and hear. If I like what comes out, I might decide to develop it further. If I don't, it goes into the "save for later" file, when I might feel differently about what I wrote or see something I missed the first time around.

Here are some of my favorite, can't-miss prompts, collected over the years from writing exercises, my own drafts, and workshops. Try one. You might just be surprised and delighted with what you create.

- *Start with "I was [insert age] by then and . . ."*
- *Think of a favorite song or prayer. Pick a line from it and use that line three times in your writing.*

- *Start with "The truth is . . ." or "This is what I could not tell you . . ." or "You don't really know me until you know this . . ."*
- *Start with "There is the moment everything changes . . ."*
- *Find a copy of the poem "Where I'm From" by George Ella Lyon or "Wild Geese" by Mary Oliver. Use them as springboards to write about your roots or to write an ethical will (a piece that shares your values) for your children.*
- *Start with any one of these words—home, hands, rosary, mirror, matchbox—or try using more than one in the same piece.*
- *Find a quiet corner and close your eyes. Wait for an image or memory. Stay with it awhile. Observe as if the memory is playing out on stage. Who is there? Who is not there? What is happening? You are invisible to what is going on—so if you were to walk onto that stage, what would you touch, smell, notice on the walls or in the room? Now write.*

Keep in Mind

- There is no wrong way to write your memoir.
- Have fun with telling your stories in your natural voice, as if you were telling them to a friend or trusted confidante. This is not the time to be worried about spelling, punctuation, or grammar. This is the time to get your stories on the page (or computer screen)!
- A memoir doesn't have to be a full accounting of everything that ever happened to you—and probably shouldn't be. The most interesting

memoirs are the ones told in your own voice about the events, large and small, that happened to you and what they meant or how they shaped the person you became.

- Your one voice, vulnerable and true, is enough to make an impact on your audience.

- You can write something meaningful even in a short amount of time. Think about just doing a number of short writings over a few weeks; often you'll find a theme emerging that can be the heart of a longer memoir. But even if not, these "mini-memoirs" will still be treasured keepsakes.

- If you are having trouble getting started on writing your memoir, try starting with one prompt at a time.

- Draft freely. Then when you're ready, dive in and tell your story.

Appendix B
PRINT AND DIGITAL RESOURCES FOR GOING FURTHER

Chapter 1: Memoir Your Way

Internet Resource

personalhistorians.org

Members of the Association of Personal Historians (APH) help individuals, families, organizations, and communities preserve their life stories. If you feel that the task of collecting your life stories is daunting, or if you'd like to capture the stories of your family elders but are pressed for time, you can contact an APH member for guidance. APH members are skilled at helping people develop their own personal history projects. They use techniques such as recording audio or video interviews, transcribing interviews into written form, and/or collating family photos and documents into an edited and custom-designed and -published product. Many APH members also do community or organizational histories or oral histories. Their website lists resources for those who might want to contribute their personal histories to national historical archives such as StoryCorps or the Veterans History Project.

Chapter 2: Five Simple Steps to Telling a True Story

Books

Fletcher, Ralph. *How to Write Your Life Story*. New York: HarperCollins, 2007.

——. *Live Writing: Breathing Life into Your Words*. New York: Avon Books, 1999.

Norton, Lisa Dale. *Shimmering Images: A Handy Little Guide to Writing Memoir*. New York: St. Martin's Griffin, 2008.

Rainer, Tristine. *Your Life as Story*. New York: Putnam, 1998.

Silverman, Sue William. *Fearless Confessions: A Writer's Guide to Memoir*. Athens, GA: University of Georgia Press, 2009.

Thomas, Abigail. *Thinking About Memoir*. New York: Sterling for AARP, 2008.

Internet Sources/Resources

www.youtube.com/watch?v=aioru6ce3Nc

Part of the series "Writers on Writing," this brief interview with E. Ethelbert Miller discusses two different approaches to memoir that writers can take, and gives examples of each from Miller's published work.

freelance-writing.lovetoknow.com/Tips_on_Writing_a_Memoir *and*

www.rd.com/advice/great-tips-on-how-to-write-your-memoir

General tips on writing memoir

leemartinauthor.com/blog/2014/11/the-layers-of-memoir

Here, author Lee Martin shows how to get at the deeper insights that make a memoir not only memorable, but meaningful.

Chapter 3: Around the Table: Food and Cookbook Memoirs

Books

Bhide, Monica. *A Life of Spice*. CreateSpace Independent Publishing Platform, 2015. *(She also has a blog and an app. www.MonicaBhide.com. Phone app: iSpice. Bhide writes about Indian food and also writes about parenting, publishing, and social media.)*

Karim, Kay. *The Iraqi Family Cookbook*. Hippocrene Books, 2011. *(Karim began writing her family cookbook in the evening after her day's work as a librarian in Virginia. She grew up in Iraq and moved to the United States after she married.)*

Kurlansky, Mark. *The Food of a Younger Land*. New York: Riverhead, 2009.

Ziegelman, Jane. *97 Orchard Street: An Edible History of Five Immigrant Families in One New York Tenement*. New York: Harper Paperbacks, May 2011.

Internet Resources

www.BlogHerFood.com

A platform for women bloggers who have a combined audience of 92 million women through blogs and social media. Well over half the blogs feature food and recipes.

www.chowdc.org and www.culinaryhistoriansannarbor.org

Look for culinary history groups, including Culinary Historians of Washington, DC, or Culinary Historians of Ann Arbor, MI.

www.KitchenSisters.org

"Hidden Kitchens" is a radio series that airs on National Public Radio's *Morning Edition*. The Kitchen Sisters, Davia Nelson and Nikki Silva, explore the world of unexpected, below the radar cooking, legendary meals, and eating traditions—how communities come together through food. "Hidden Kitchens" travels the country chronicling American kitchen cultures and hidden kitchens around the world, past and present.

www.orangette.net

Molly Wizenberg began her blog in 2004. She has written about food, marriage, having a child, living in Seattle, writing books, and opening a restaurant with her husband.

www.thepioneerwoman.com

In 2006 Ree Drummond began a food blog about her experiences as she transitioned from city girl to wife and mother on a cattle ranch in Oklahoma. From those recipes, photos, and life stories, she started writing cookbooks, such as *The Pioneer Woman Cooks: Recipes from an Accidental Country Girl.*

www.101cookbooks.com/archives/writing-a-cookbook-proposal-recipe .html

Heidi Swanson, author of *Near & Far: Recipes Inspired by Home and Travel,* wrote this article about creating a cookbook proposal. Although she wrote this for writers who plan to publish their cookbooks, she summarizes ideas and decisions that clarify the thought process for anyone planning to create a family cookbook. The 101 Cookbooks website is helpful also for reviewing a wide variety of cookbook themes and styles.

Chapter 4: Reinvent Your Scrapbook

Books

Best, Laura. *Scrapbooking Your Family History*. New York: Sterling/Chapelle, 2007.

Governo, Tara (ed.). *Imperfect Lives: Scrapbooking the Reality of Your Everyday*. Cincinnati: Memory Makers, 2006.

Wines-Read, Jeanne and Joan Wines. *Scrapbooking for Dummies*. Indianapolis: Wiley, 2004.

——. *Digital Scrapbooking for Dummies*. Indianapolis: Wiley, 2005.

Internet Sources/Resources

www.paperwishes.com

This "Scrapbooking 101" guide is a great resource. Especially check out the article "Creating Masculine Scrapbook Pages" at this link: www.paper-wishes.com/scrapbooking101/articles/creating-masculine-scrapbook-pages.html

www.loc.gov/pictures

"Prints & Photographs Online Catalog." Library of Congress.

www.publicdomainpictures.net

"Public Domain Pictures." Bobek Inc, 2007–2015.

Chapter 5: Create Your Memoir as a Graphic Novel

Internet Resources

Your Search Engine (Google, Bing, Yahoo)

When using the search bar, be specific with your keywords. Type in more detailed terms than "graphic novels." Successful search keywords include: graphic novels how to, how to create a graphic novel, graphic novel creation process, drawing for graphic novels.

www.youtube.com

After Google, YouTube is the largest internet research library, and that includes graphic novels. You can enjoy videos about the creation process and the production process as well as videos made by your favorite illustrators, creator interviews, graphic novel reviews, and promo videos. You can even find background music for drawing if you'd like some musical inspiration. The same suggested keywords above apply here.

www.spxpo.com

The Small Press Expo is "North America's premiere independent cartooning and comic arts festival." It's smaller and very different from all the Comic-Cons that take up entire convention centers. Graphic novels and their creators from all stages of life, plus their publishers, are prominently featured at the festival, which includes the Expo floor, panels, award ceremony, and classes. Thousands of graphic novel fans show up for the festival every fall in Bethesda, Maryland, to meet their favorite graphic novel creators and buy books.

www.worldcat.org

Your public library is also a great place to find popular graphic novels. Here's why: unlike comic books, which are mostly inexpensive, graphic novels are sometimes as pricy as hardcover books. Public libraries love graphic novels due to their high circulation rates, which in turn help boost library budgets. It's the best resource for reading or simply skimming through a bunch of graphic novels. Look in person at your local library, online on your local branch site, or on WorldCat, the world's largest network of library content and services. Items not available locally may sometimes be borrowed from other systems via Interlibrary Loan (ILL).

Chapter 6: Memory Quilts – A Way to Celebrate Lives

Books

Bonsib, Sandy. *Memory Quilts: 20 Heartwarming Projects with Special Techniques.* Chanhassen, MN: Creative Publishing International, 2004.

Buckley, Karen K. *Above and Beyond Basics: A Medley of Quilted Memoirs.* Paducah, KY: Collector Books, 1996.

DeLeonandis, Martha. *T-Shirt Quilts Made Easy.* Paducah, KY: American Quilter's Society, 2012.

Hale, Sue. *Memories on Fabric.* Concord, California: C & T Publishing, 2007.

Leisure Arts. *Memory Quilts with T-Shirts, Autographs & Photos.* Better Homes and Gardens Creative Collection. Maumelle, Arizona: Leisure Arts, 2007.

Richards, Rhonda. *Memory Quilts in the Making.* Oxmoor House, 1999.

Smiley, Jan Bode. *The Art of Fabric Books.* Concord, California: C & T Publishing, 2011.

Trulaske, Sarah. *A Quilted Memoir.* St. Louis, MO: Simple Abundance Press, 2011.

Internet Resource

www.yourstorymatters.com/video.html

Carlyn Saltman, personal historian and award-winning documentary videographer, talks about memoir videos.

Chapter 7: Nurturing the Young Storyteller
Books

AARP. *Conversations with My Father: A Keepsake Journal for Celebrating a Lifetime of Stories.* Lark Crafts, 2007.

Flournoy, Valerie. *The Patchwork Quilt.* Dial,1985. *(In this children's book about family legacy, Tanya's grandmother is making a memory quilt with pieces of clothing from the whole family.)*

Lashier, Kathleen. *Grandma, Tell Me Your Memories.* Heirloom edition. G & R Publishing: 2012. *(A journal with ready-made interview questions.)*

Morris, Ann. *Grandma Francisca Remembers: A Hispanic-American Family Story*. Minneapolis, MN: Millbrook Press, 2002. Other titles in Ann Morris's "What Was It Like Grandma?" Series include:

Grandma Esther Remembers: A Jewish-American Family Story

Grandma Lai Goon Remembers: A Chinese-American Family Story

Grandma Lois Remembers: An African-American Family Story

Grandma Maxine Remembers: A Native American Family Story

Grandma Susan Remembers: A British-American Family Story

Grandma Hekmatt Remembers: An Arab-American Family Story

Wollman-Bonilla, Julie. *Family Message Journals: Teaching Writing through Family Involvement*. National Council of Teachers of English, 2000. *(This book supports the premise that writing begins at home.)*

Internet Resources

www.literacyinlearningexchange.org/storytelling-primer

The Literacy in Learning Exchange offers a free downloadable "Storytelling Primer" that explains the role of storytelling traditions and provides reflective questions for storytellers.

www.readwritethink.org

ReadWriteThink is a website created by the International Literacy Association/National Council of Teachers of English as a resource on storytelling for parents and educators.

www.yesalliance.org

The Youth, Educators, and Storytelling Alliance is a special interest group of the national storytelling network.

Chapter 8: You Are the Bridge – Traditions and Heritage

Internet Resources

www.pbs.org/kenburns

Ken Burns's documentaries and television documentary miniseries, such as *The Dust Bowl*, *Jazz*, *The Statue of Liberty*, and *Baseball* give vivid histories of American life.

"How To" Dance Videos on Youtube

Search for the name of a dance from your heritage and you will find videos teaching basic through advanced dance steps. The videos can vary in quality and authenticity, but watching some of them is an easy way to get a feel for the moves and music of your family's history. These videos of bhangra and bollywood steps are examples of what you can find:

www.youtube.com/watch?v=mVhfaPpxDkw A woman dance instructor teaches a combination of basic bhangra and bollywood dance steps.

www.youtube.com/watch?v=bkfHp0HJSMs A group of men practice bhangra dance steps.

www.storycorps.org

StoryCorps is a nonprofit organization that records short interviews that are broadcast on National Public Radio. Their website has a good list of possible interview questions (storycorps.org/great-questions).

www.census.gov

The United States Census Bureau's website features current census information, interactive maps, and sixty-second audio daily news information on everything from June brides to household pets. Start with these quick links:

Daily Audio Features: www.census.gov/library/audio/profile-america.html

Landing Page for Visualizations and Infographics: www.census.gov/library.html

www.loc.gov

The Library of Congress is the nation's oldest federal cultural institution and serves as the research arm of Congress. It is also the largest library in the world, with millions of books, recordings, photographs, maps, and manuscripts in its collections. Special categories include "Veterans History Project" (collecting, preserving, and presenting memories of American war veterans), "Chronicling America" (millions of newspaper pages back to 1836), "The National Jukebox" (music and historical recordings), and "Local Legacies" (a 2010 report on the creative arts, crafts, and customs representing traditional community life in all fifty states plus territories). You can also visit the LOC in person in Washington, DC.

www.archives.gov

The US National Archives and Records Administration (NARA) houses historical census records from 1790 through 1940. On their site, you can investigate documents such as immigration records, naturalization papers, census schedules, draft cards, homestead applications, and records about Native Americans, early settlers from Europe, and many other population groups. You can also visit the National Archives in person at one of their many locations, including the Washington, DC, headquarters. Start with these quick links:

Resources for Genealogists: www.archives.gov/research/genealogy

Online Resource Tools: www.archives.gov/research/start/online-tools.html

www.si.edu

The Smithsonian Institution in Washington, DC, is a complex of several amazing museums such as the American History Museum, the Air and Space Museum, the African Art Museum, and many others. The Smithsonian is also home to the Smithsonian Center for Folklife and Cultural Heritage (folklife.si.edu), which is a huge gathering of American folklore and folk music, including their nonprofit record label, Folkways Recordings. Listen to blues, gospel, Celtic, Asian, and down-home music from wherever your home happens to be. (folkways.si.edu)